Physical Characteristics of the Toy Fox Terrier

(from the American Kennel Club's breed standard)

The topline is level when standing and gaiting. The body is balanced and tapers slightly from ribs ank. The chest is deep and muscular with well sprung ribs. The back is straight, level, and muscular. and strong in loin with moderate tuck-up. The croup is level with topline and well-rounded.

Tail: Set high, held erect and in proportion to the size of the dog. Docked to the third or fourth joint.

Hindquarters: Well angulated, strong and muscular. The upper and lower thighs are strong, well muscled and of good length. The stifles are clearly defined and well angulated. Hock joints are well let down and firm. The rear pasterns are straight. The legs are parallel from the rear

Color: Tri-color: Predominately black head with sharply defined tan markings on cheeks, lips and eye dots. White, Chocolate and Tan: Predominately chocolate head with sharply defined tan markings on cheeks, lips and eye dots. White and Tan: Predominately tan head. White and Black: Predominately black head. (Note: In all colors, body is over 50% white, with or without body spots.)

Size: 8.5–11.5 inches,
9–11 preferred,
8.5–11.5 acceptable.

Feet: Small and oval, pointing forward. Toes are strong, well-arched and closely knit with deep pads.

Toy Fox Terrier

By Richard G. Beauchamp

Contents

Training Your Toy Fox Terrier 86

By Charlotte Schwartz
Be informed about the importance of training your Toy Fox Terrier from the basics of housebreaking and understanding the development of a young dog to executing obedience commands (sit, stay, down, etc.).

Health Care of Your Toy Fox Terrier 107

Discover how to select a qualified vet and care for your dog at all stages of life. Topics include vaccinations, skin problems, dealing with external and internal parasites and common medical and behavioral conditions.

Showing Your Toy Fox Terrier 138

Enter the world of showing dogs. Learn about the two major dog clubs, the United Kennel Club and the American Kennel Club, the different types of shows and the making of a champion. Go beyond the conformation ring to agility trials, obedience trials and more.

Behavior of Your Toy Fox Terrier 146

Learn to recognize and handle behavioral problems that may arise with your Toy Fox Terrier. Topics discussed include separation anxiety, aggression, barking, chewing, digging, begging, jumping up and more.

KENNEL CLUB BOOKS® TOY FOX TERRIER
ISBN: 1-59378-403-1

Copyright © 2003, 2006 • Kennel Club Books, LLC
308 Main Street, Allenhurst, NJ 07711 USA
Cover Design Patented: US 6,435,559 B2 • Printed in South Korea

Photographs by Mary Bloom, with additional photos by:
Norvia Behling, TJ Calhoun, Carolina Biological Supply, Doskocil, Isabelle Français, James Hayden-Yoav, RBP, Carol Ann Johnson, Bill Jonas, Dwight R. Kuhn, Dr. Dennis Kunkel, Mikki Pet Products, Phototake, Jean Claude Revy and Dr. Andrew Spielman.

Illustrations by Patricia Peters.

The publisher would like to thank all of the owners of the dogs featured in this book, including Karen Brancheau, Samantha Gershman, Dori Hallaway, Margi Hill, Paula Hradkowsky, Mary Ranieri, Alexandra Van Horne and Diane Van Horne.

Considered to be an American breed through and through, the Toy Fox Terrier (once called the AmerToy) derives entirely from British stock.

HISTORY OF THE
TOY FOX TERRIER

What a never-ending series of contradictions this smart-looking little fellow is! The Toy Fox Terrier is a "new kid on the block" when it comes to the American Kennel Club's registry, and at the same time the breed's name has practically been a household word in the US for over half of a century. There's no doubt at all that the Toy Fox Terrier is an "all-American" product, but his roots are entirely British. And even at that, although his ancestors came directly from the British Isles, he's all but unknown there.

Now, after all these years, the Toy Fox Terrier may just become the dog *du jour* on the American show scene. So, what about this "new" little breed? Just what is his story? To fully understand how this delightful little companion dog came to be what he is today, we must skip back in time—way back!

ORIGIN OF THE TERRIERS

If we travel back to about 3500 to 2000 BC, we find that, among the descendants of the rugged Northern wolf, a rather distinct group of dogs to which the Toy Fox Terrier owes his earliest beginnings had evolved. This group produced many of the small breeds that were developed in the Neolithic lake-dwellings of the northernmost regions of Europe. This family was known as *Canis familiaris palustris* or, more commonly and interchangeably, as "the dog of the lake" and "the peat bog dog."

Although the exact role of these dogs in regard to the tribes with which they lived remains unknown, it is believed that they may have served as what we have come to think of as watchdogs—those who sound the alarm by barking when danger threatens. The alert nature, rapid vocal response and protective devotion to home and hearth of the descen-

dants of these dogs certainly give credibility to this theory.

The dog was also used by the Neolithic pile-dwelling people to follow and confront foxes and badgers in their holes. The lithe build, aggressive nature and lightning-fast responses of the dogs made them particularly suitable for hunting small vermin.

From this original source, crossed with a good number of other breeds already in existence, many new breeds were eventually developed—among them the terrier breeds that were developed in Europe; more specifically, in England, Scotland and Ireland. These terrier dogs retained the smaller size, mercurial nature and lightning speed of their spitz ancestors and were similarly extremely devoted to their owners.

This tiny fox, known as the bat-eared fox, *Otocyon megalotis*, barely reaches 12 pounds, but more usually 7 pounds, comparable to the size of Toy Fox Terriers today. The Toy Fox's larger cousins were named for their skill at hunting fox.

Liberia $20

BAT-EARED FOX *Otocyon megalotis*

They required little space, were hardy and kept the vermin population in check.

Among the many variations of these terrier dogs, there were those that were looked upon as having no fear of any other living animal. Sydenham Edwards, a noted sporting authority and author of the 19th century, had a great deal to say about these dogs in *Cynographia Britannica*, which was published in 1800: "The terrier is querulous, fretful, irascible, high spirited and alert when brought into action; it is not what he will bear, but what he will inflict. His action protects himself and his bite carries death to his opponents...He dashes into the hole of the fox, drives him from his recesses, or tears him to pieces in his stronghold; and he forces the reluctant, stubborn badger into light. He will trace with the foxhounds, hunt with beagle, find for the greyhound, or beat with the spaniel."

Between the years 1800 and 1805, a great number of sporting books and works on hunting and dogs was published, all of which dealt more or less with terriers. Many of the terriers were described as being black with tan legs, tan muzzles and a spot of the same over each eye. There was an occasional reddish fawn. White dogs with spotted markings were at first rare but were to grow increasingly popular. Some were

GENUS *CANIS*
Dogs and wolves are members of the genus *Canis*. Wolves are known scientifically as *Canis lupus* while dogs are known as *Canis domesticus*. Dogs and wolves are known to interbreed. The term "canine" derives from the Latin-derived word *Canis*. The term "dog" has no scientific basis but has been used for thousands of years. The origin of the word "dog" has never been authoritatively ascertained.

rough-coated, others smooth.

On some dogs, the ears were small and sometimes erect. It is interesting to note that the ears and part of the tails of many of the dogs were cut off. This was undoubtedly done to give their quarry less purchase when it came to a confrontation.

Size varied widely, with most falling in the 10–20-pound range. Stonehenge, however, who was a noted dog author of the day, wrote of terriers that ranged in weight between 6–10 pounds and still others who would weigh as much as 20 pounds. However, it appears that most authorities of that time readily agreed that dogs above that size were too big to effectively pursue their quarry.

The success of several strains of these dogs in the sport of fox hunting had long since earned them the name "Fox Terrier," and the earliest known picture of a dog referred to by that name was Colonel Thornton's Pitch, a prick-eared white dog with black head marks and a spot at the root of the tail.

By the time that Fox Terriers had begun to attract the public's attention in the mid-1800s, most of the dogs were white and they were seen in both rough and smooth coats. It appears that when they began to make their appearance at dog shows, the smart clean lines of the smoother-coated dogs had great appeal.

The first class ever offered for Fox Terriers was in June 1862 at

Note the small terrier-like dogs frolicking in the foreground of this famous Flemish painting.

the North of England Second Exhibition of Sporting and Other Dogs show held in the Agricultural Hall, Islington, London. A black and tan marked dog named "Trimmer" from Colonel Arkwright's Oakley Hunt strain defeated an entry of 20.

The following year, however, was a historic point in the development of the Fox Terrier because the entry of the Birmingham show included three Fox Terriers—Old Jock, Old Trap and Tartar—who were destined to become the foundation of the breed as we know it today. It is appears to be conclusively believed by all involved in the breed that all Fox Terriers, smooth-coated or wire, trace back to these three dogs. The trio is also credited with stimulating the interest that ignited the meteoric rise to popularity of the Fox Terrier in England and then the rest of the world.

It is worth noting here that at the same time that interest in the Fox Terrier was blossoming, prominent dog writers frequently made reference to the "diminutive toy terriers" that had become highly fashionable with the ladies of the day. Both Stonehenge in *Dogs of Great Britain, America and Other Countries* and Hugh Dalziel in *British Dogs*, Volume II, gave considerable attention to the little dogs.

Both authors made mention of

WHITE IN THE COAT

The early Fox Terriers in England were predominantly brown or tan with black markings. White spotted or whole white dogs were rare. However, it was the masters of England's hunt kennels who popularized the white dogs. They realized that the hounds, bent on the chase, could mistake the darker terriers for the fox in their hunting frenzy. The white Fox Terrier made it easier for both hound and hunter to tell the difference.

The King Charles Spaniel was crossbred into the small Fox Terrier, unfortunately resulting in dogs with undesirable "apple" heads.

The elegant Italian Greyhound contributed its petite size to the Toy Fox Terrier, but also introduced the rounded topline, which is not desirable in the Toy Fox.

the difficulties encountered in breeding dogs of typical quality that were also of the highly desirable small size. Breeders resorted to the use of the King Charles Spaniel and Italian Greyhound to reduce size. Unfortunately, as the authors indicated, use of the King Charles resulted in "apple-headed 'uns" and those from the Italian Greyhound crosses showed "the wheel back and tucked up flank" of the Italian Greyhound.

There were also very small dogs born among the Fox Terriers that came from more conventional stock. Collectively, the small Fox Terriers amounted to sufficient numbers to warrant some talk of classes just for them at the time, but their popularity remained solely with the general public and not among the show aficionados.

THE FOX TERRIER SAILS THE ATLANTIC

"Tort," a smooth-coated Fox Terrier bitch, is given official credit as the first of her kind to be sent to America, arriving at the close of the 1870s. She was soon followed by other exports from England's leading breeders of the day.

The Fox Terrier was no less well received in America than it had been in Great Britain. By 1885, many highly regarded and influential dog men of the day had become interested in the breed. Through their efforts, the American Fox Terrier Club was founded.

The foregoing is the official history of the Fox Terrier's early days in America. But at the same time we can only surmise that there was more than one emigrant from the British Isles who was not about to embark on his journey to the US without his treasured family dog. So, while Tort may be given official recognition as the first of her kind to arrive in America, this says nothing of the many Fox Terriers who undoubtedly sailed the Atlantic and took up residence in the United States without note. And if the "diminutive toy terriers" existed in Britain, their home country, they were just as likely to have been stowed away on journeys to America.

While the official exports thrived on the American show scene, the smaller dogs seemed to have a unique charm all their own that particularly suited the purposes of dog lovers across America. The little dogs fulfilled the needs of those who wanted a home companion that was small enough and affordable enough for even the most humble dwelling. The dogs were clever, easily taught and affectionate, and the ladies of the household loved them because they got along with everyone in the family.

Capping off all of their

RISE TO POPULARITY

The first separate classes for Fox Terriers in Great Britain were offered in 1863. Entries were negligible at best. Within ten short years of that time, the Fox Terrier had moved from obscurity on the British show scene to remarkable celebrity. There were 276 Fox Terriers entered at the Nottingham show in 1872. The breed, and particularly the Smooth variety, grew from strength to strength and, just two years after The Kennel Club was established in 1876, the Fox Terrier Club was founded. The Fox Terrier Club followed the establishment of England's oldest specialty club, that for Bulldogs, by only one year.

charm, intelligence and convenient diminutive size was a unique ability to keep the vermin population under control. The little

COMPANY LOGO
The great popularity of the Fox Terrier in America prompted the RCA Victor Company to use the breed as part of its logo. "His Master's Voice" pictures a black and white Smooth Fox Terrier cocking his head and listening intently from the sounds emerging from one of the company's "victrolas." The picture remains a highly identifiable symbol to this day.

Fox Terrier, unlike many other small breeds, had hunting instincts that even earned it the respect of the men of the family. Who could not appreciate the pluck and lightning speed with which the little dogs could dispatch vermin indoors and out! Thus the "runts" of the Fox Terrier world took on a persona of their own and earned a name and respect for themselves totally apart from that reserved by the

dog-show-going public for the larger specimens of the breed. Individuals across the country began intentionally breeding for the smaller size. In some sections of the country, the small dogs were known as "Fyce" or "Fiest" dogs—a name so given due to their plucky and fiesty natures.

In 1915, some breeders of the little terriers approached the American Kennel Club (AKC) in hopes of having the dogs registered there. Their application to have the dogs accepted as a separate and distinct breed from their larger ancestors was rejected.

Disappointed but not disheartened, the dedicated breeders turned to the United Kennel Club (UKC) for assistance. The UKC had been founded by Chauncey Z. Bennett in 1898, just a few years after the AKC had opened its doors. The UKC had already begun to register Smooth Fox Terriers in 1912. The organization agreed to accept the smaller dogs into their registry, but simply as Smooth Fox Terriers rather than as a separate breed.

What followed was constant struggle and indecision among the breeders on the subject of size. The supporters of the small dogs realized that achieving their goal as a separate toy breed was hopeless in so long as they were a part of, and using, the larger Smooth Fox Terrier in their breeding programs.

By 1920, the group initiated their appeal to the UKC for separate breed status, but their cause was hard won and it was not until 1936 that the UKC awarded separate and distinct status to the dogs as Toy Fox Terriers. The first litter, of just a single puppy, was registered under that breed name on February 24, 1936. The Toy Fox Terrier was on its way.

THE EARLY YEARS

Most dog breeders will quickly agree that it is much easier to breed a good large dog than it is to breed a good small dog. This was no less true for the Toy Fox Terrier and, as it has in countless other breeds in their formative years, ideal size quickly became a point of disagreement.

From the beginning of mankind's putting its hand to the breeding of dogs, it has been apparent that development of any breed required objectivity and ingenuity. Often this came in the form of resorting to crossing out to an already well-established breed to introduce a desired characteristic into the new breed being developed.

There is no written documentation of the introduction of Chihuahua or Toy Manchester Terrier blood into the breeding programs of the rapidly developing Toy Fox Terrier. However, it is generally accepted among many long-time breeders that this is so. Even casual observation of the differences that exist between today's Smooth and Toy Fox Terriers would indicate that some intervention other than simple selectivity would have to have taken place.

Undoubtedly for this and other important reasons, it became apparent a few years after the Toy Fox's recognition that, in

Today's Smooth Fox Terrier, one of the world's most recognizable pure-bred dogs, is the obvious progenitor of the Toy Fox Terrier breed.

The Toy Manchester Terrier, also known as the English Toy Terrier, is believed to have been crossbred with the Toy Fox.

The Chihuahua, without competition the world's smallest pure-bred dog, likely contributed to the development of the Toy Fox Terrier.

order to develop consistency in the breed and provide leadership, a central authority for the Toy Fox Terrier had to be established. On August 31, 1949, Dr. E. G. Fuhrman called together a small group of diehard Toy Fox Terrier fanciers to organize a breed club devoted solely to the best interests of the breed. A constitution and by-laws were drafted, ushering in the National Toy Fox Terrier Association (NTFTA).

Over the following ten years, the NTFTA was tireless in its efforts to establish breeding guidelines and standards of excellence for the breed. Their hard-won success in doing so was rewarded by the UKC on August 31, 1960, when the UKC closed the official stud book to registration of any Toy Fox Terrier other than those bred from dogs already included.

No more positive step could have been taken on the breed's behalf. Through the efforts of fanciers breeding under the auspices of the NTFTA and the UKC, the Toy Fox Terrier as we know it today was developed. The following years brought ever-increasing uniformity in the breed and gave birth to the rise of several bloodlines predominant in respect to quality and consistency. The Toy Fox Terrier remains among the UKC's top dogs in terms of registrations, outnumbering all other toy breeds (though it is officially shown in the Terrier Group). In 2004 the breed ranked number 12.

QUEST FOR AKC RECOGNITION

In 1994, successful Toy Fox Terrier breeder and exhibitor Chrystyne Gettman began to contact and organize breeders throughout the country who shared her interest in obtaining additional recognition for the Toy Fox Terrier through AKC acceptance. Finding enthusiastic national support, a meeting was held in Yakima, Washington that same year and the group established the American Toy Fox Terrier Club (ATFTC). Chrystyne Gettman was elected president. Diana Morse was named custodian of the organization's registry.

In 1998, the naming of Mike Massey as president and Laura Perkinson as liaison to the AKC marked accelerated efforts in respect to AKC recognition. With the assistance and support of the entire membership, their efforts were rewarded. The Toy Fox Terrier was admitted to the Miscellaneous Class of the AKC on April 1, 2001. Further progress was made as the breed and its proponents received their ultimate goal: full recognition of the Toy Fox Terrier as a member of the AKC's Toy Group beginning January 1, 2003.

What an incredible journey

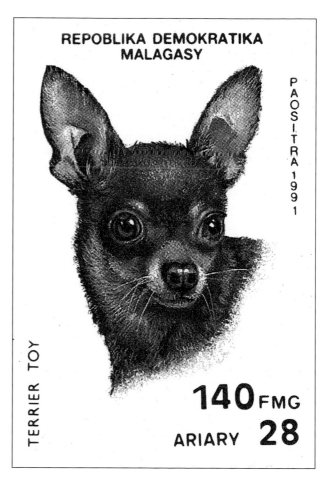

this breed has taken since the days of Colonel Thornton's Pitch, Colonel Arkwright's Trimmer and that portentous trio of Old Jock, Old Trap and Tartar at the Birmingham show in England. Certainly, the Toy Fox Terrier is an American breed, but it goes without saying that England can take a bow for having produced such a solid foundation upon which the breed is based.

Toy Terriers are revered around the world, as shown in this postage stamp from the Malagasy Republic (currently Madagascar).

CHARACTERISTICS OF THE

TOY FOX TERRIER

Before anyone tries to decide whether or not the Toy Fox Terrier is the correct breed for him, a larger, more important, question must be asked. That question is, "Should I own a dog at all?" Do not assume that the diminutive size of the breed eliminates work and responsibility. On the contrary, all dogs, large or small, demand

"Is this breed good with children?" Provided that the children are well behaved and taught how to correctly handle a small dog, this is an excellent choice for a family with children.

commitment and consistency. They are not like some hobbies that you can put away on a shelf until you get back "in the mood."

Dog ownership, regardless of breed, is a serious and time-consuming responsibility that should not be entered into lightly. Failure to understand this can make sheer drudgery out of what should be a rewarding relationship. It is also one of the primary reasons that thousands upon thousands of unwanted dogs end their lives on the streets or as the wards of humane societies and animal shelters.

If the prospective dog owner lives alone and environmental conditions are conducive to dog ownership, all that person needs to do is be sure that he has a strong desire to make the necessary commitment that dog ownership entails. In the case of family households, however, the situation is a much more complicated one. It is vital that the person who will actually be responsible for the dog's care truly wants a dog. In many households, the additional responsibility of caring for the family pets often falls on one member of the family. Children are away at school all day. In many families, both parents work, but often it is one of the parents who is saddled with the additional chores of house-breaking, feeding and trips to the vet. What was supposed to be a family affair eventually becomes another responsibility for one family member!

Nearly all children love puppies and dogs, and will promise anything to get one. But childhood enthusiasm can wane very quickly and it will be up to the adults in the family to ensure that the dog receives proper care. Children should be taught responsibility with regards to owning a pet, but to expect a living, breathing and needy animal to teach a child this lesson is incredibly indifferent to the needs of the animal.

In the case of toy breeds and toddlers, common sense must be employed. A very young child cannot be expected to understand the care required in handling these small dogs. On the other hand, with proper instruction, children old enough to understand how to handle a small dog can learn to enjoy the exuberant personality of the Toy Fox Terrier and the dog in turn will love gentle children.

There are also many households in which the entire family is gone from early morning until late in the day. The question that must be asked, then, is who will provide

CROWD FAVORITES
During the 1920s and on through the days of the Great Depression in America, there was little money available for entertainment. Traveling road shows surviving on voluntary contributions or admissions of a few pennies became popular. More often than not, trick-dog acts shared the billing with other acts, and the tiny Fox Terriers proved especially entertaining in this respect. They quickly became crowd favorites from coast to coast.

food for the dog and give him access to the outdoors for house-breaking? An adult dog can wait to relieve himself for longer periods of time, but it is totally unfair for anyone to expect a young puppy to be left alone (and to "hold it") for the entire day.

Should an individual or family find that they are capable of providing the proper home for a dog or young puppy, suitability of breed must also be considered. If you are willing to make the necessary commitment that a Toy Fox

Terrier requires, let us assure you that there are few breeds that are more amiable and adaptable to an owner's home.

LIFE WITH A TOY FOX TERRIER
Although the Toy Fox is of diminutive size, the breed has an amazing constitution and surprising energy

ON-LEASH ONLY

A Toy Fox Terrier should always be on-leash and under control when not in the safe confines of your home. The breed's curiosity can lead to complete disregard for rules and training—what he sees on the other side of the street may call more loudly than your voice. Likewise, the Toy Fox Terrier is not beyond flinging himself at a passing Doberman Pinscher or Great Dane in order to protect you.

and endurance. When purchased from a responsible breeder, the Toy Fox Terrier is unique among dogs in that the breed is seldom prone to chronic illnesses or genetic infirmities. The breed is able to maintain this cheerful, healthy constitution well on into old age. This is not a happy accident. Serious breeders make mental and physical soundness a top priority, and it shows in the dogs that they breed.

The Toy Fox Terrier is extremely playful and inquisitive. You will quickly find that he never ceases to have something to do. At the same time, this is a breed that enjoys snuggling up by your side as much as you might enjoy having him do so.

Although the breed has not lost its hunting instinct, introduced early enough and properly supervised, the Toy Fox Terrier can coexist with your cat or rabbit as well as he can with humans. Compatibility with small rodents and birds may take some time and patience, but nothing is impossible.

Very few members of the breed are particularly dog-aggressive and few, if any, have problems with another dog in the household as long as the two are introduced properly. This is particularly so if they are of the opposite sex. The Toy Fox Terrier is a breed of which it can be said without hesitation that two are just as easy to raise as one.

MALE OR FEMALE?

The sex of a dog in many breeds is a very important consideration, but this is not really the case with the Toy Fox Terrier. The male Toy Fox Terrier makes just as loving, devoted and trainable of a companion as does the female. In fact, there are a good many owners who believe a male can be even more devoted to his master than the female.

There is one important point to consider in determining your choice between male and female. Although both must be trained not to relieve themselves anywhere in the home, unneutered male Toy Fox Terriers have the natural instinct to lift their legs and urinate to "mark" their home territories. It seems confusing to many dog owners, but a male's marking his home turf has absolutely nothing to do with whether or not he is housebroken. The two responses come from entirely different needs and must be dealt with in that manner. Some dogs are more difficult to train not to mark territory in the house than others. Males that are used for breeding are even more prone to this behavior and are even harder to break of it.

On the other hand, unspayed females have their semiannual heat cycles once they have reached sexual maturity. In the case of the female Toy Fox Terrier, this can occur for the first time at about ten months of age, but it can take place

Every dog responds to one-on-one interaction, and the Toy Fox Terrier will reach his potential if he is encouraged and loved on a very regular basis.

a month or two earlier or later. The heat cycles will recur every six to nine months, depending upon the individual female.

Heat cycles are accompanied by a vaginal discharge that creates the need to confine the female for about three weeks so that she does not soil her surroundings. It must be understood that the female has no control over this discharge, so it has nothing to do with training.

Most Toy Fox Terrier are not left outdoors by themselves for long periods of time, but this is especially true when the female is in heat. During her cycle, she should not be outdoors alone even for a brief moment or two. The need for confinement and keeping a careful watch over the female in heat is especially important to prevent her becoming pregnant by some neighborhood Lothario.

LITTLE ATHLETE
The Toy Fox Terrier stands among the most athletic of the smaller breeds. The breed consistently proves that competitive events like agility and flyball come as second nature. It is important, however, always to remember that the Toy Fox Terrier needs patience, understanding and a gentle touch in all his training experiences.

Especially dangerous for the female is that, as most breeds are larger than the Toy Fox, a wandering male who attempts to mate with her may be too large to actually breed her. He could seriously injure or even kill her in his attempts to do so.

The aforementioned sexually related aspects can be entirely eliminated by spaying the female and neutering the male. Unless a Toy Fox Terrier has been purchased expressly for breeding or showing from a breeder capable of making this judgment, your dog should be sexually altered. In fact, responsible breeders will insist

that the puppy destined for a home solely for pet purposes be altered at the appropriate age; this will be a part of your sales agreement.

Breeding and raising puppies should be left in the hands of people who have the facilities to keep each and every puppy in the litter until the correct homes are found. This can often take many months after a litter is born. Most dog owners are not equipped to do this. Naturally, a responsible Toy Fox Terrier owner would not allow his pet to roam the streets and end his life in an animal shelter. Unfortunately, being forced to place a puppy in a less-than-ideal home due to space or time constraints before you are able to thoroughly check out the prospective buyer may in fact create this exact situation.

Many times we have had parents ask to buy a female "just as a pet" but with full intentions of breeding so that their children can witness "the birth process." There are countless books and videos now available that portray this wonderful event and do not add to the worldwide pet overpopulation that we now face. Altering companion dogs not only precludes the possibility of adding to this problem but also eliminates bothersome behaviors in which the unaltered dog can engage.

It should be understood, however, that spaying and neutering are not reversible procedures.

Altered animals will never be able to be used for breeding.

THE TOY FOX TERRIER PERSONALITY

Many owners believe that alterations to the standard-sized Fox Terrier breed's character, through the infusion of the blood of other breeds, has resulted in a terrier that has a somewhat more tractable nature than his larger cousin. Whatever the reason, the end result is a personality that has been referred to as "terrier without trauma." But make no mistake— the Toy Fox Terrier is a terrier!

Although the Toy Fox Terrier is not, generally speaking, "dog-aggressive," don't expect yours to back down from a challenge just because the other dog is a St. Bernard or Great Dane. This fellow has no intention of stepping back when his space is invaded or his master is threatened!

The Toy Fox Terrier has lost none of the courage and spirit handed down from his earliest ancestors. The ability and desire to hunt or go to ground remain a fixed characteristic. A Toy Fox Terrier can tree squirrels and flush out rodents with the best of them.

It simply would not do for a Toy Fox Terrier to be shut away in a kennel or outdoor run with only occasional access to his owner's life and environment. Should this be your intent, you would be better

Blest with longevity, the Toy Fox Terrier can live to be a sprightly and active teenager.

served by another breed, or no dog at all! The very essence of the Toy Fox Terrier is in his unique personality and sensitive and loving nature, which are best developed by constant human contact.

We know many working

BEWARE BOREDOM!

The Toy Fox Terrier has a very high intelligence and trainability level. This can prove to be both an asset and a liability. The dog whose "schoolwork" is neglected can become a destructive and noisy nuisance. A Toy Fox Terrier has to put all that brain power somewhere and, if his owner doesn't show him how and where to put it to use, the Toy Fox Terrier's ingenuity can be astonishing.

people who are away most of the day and whose mature Toy Fox Terriers are well-mannered and trustworthy when left home alone. The key here seems to be the quality rather than quantity of time that these owners spend with their pets. Morning or evening walks, grooming sessions, game times and simply having your Toy Fox Terrier share your life when you are at home are vital to the breed's personality development and attitude. A Toy Fox Terrier likes to be talked to and praised. Like the old adage, "No man is an island," this applies to dogs as well, particularly so in the case of the Toy Fox Terrier.

We have never seen a Toy Fox Terrier even indicate that he would challenge his owner on any point, regardless of how much the dog might object to what he is being asked to do. Therefore, a stern and disapproving voice is usually more than sufficient to let your Toy Fox Terrier know that you disapprove of what he is doing. It is never

More than a space-saver in your apartment, the Toy Fox Terrier is an affectionate and courageous canine.

DON'T TALK TO STRANGERS

The average Toy Fox Terrier is more inclined to "tolerate" strangers than he is to rush out and invite them into your home. He is instinctively territorial and knows that his job is to keep a watchful eye on you and yours. Therefore, someone he knows nothing about could pose a problem in his eyes, and he will be inclined to "wait and see" rather than to welcome the person right away.

necessary to strike a Toy Fox Terrier in any circumstance. A sharp "No!" is normally more than it takes to make your point.

Don't expect your Toy Fox Terrier to assume "welcome wagon" duties in your home. Strangers are just that to the Toy Fox. Toy Fox Terriers reserve their love and affection for their owners and families and will "tolerate" outsiders if need be. Some Toy Fox Terriers will adopt one person in the family as their very own, but by and large they share their affection equally.

This is a breed that makes a great effort to please its owners and have an exceptional capacity to learn as long as its trainers is not heavy-handed. Training problems encountered are far more apt to be the fault of the owner rather than of the Toy Fox.

Setting boundaries is important to the well-being of your Toy Fox Terrier and your relationship with him. The sooner your dog understands that there are rules that must be obeyed, the easier it will be for him to become an enjoyable companion. How soon you learn to establish and enforce those rules will determine how quickly this will come about. As we mentioned earlier, the Toy Fox Terrier is not vindictive or particularly stubborn, but the breed does need guidance in order to achieve full potential.

VERSATILITY

There is no end to the number of activities you and your Toy Fox Terrier can enjoy together. The breed is highly successful in both conformation shows and obedience trials. There also are Canine Good Citizen certificates that can be earned by dogs who demonstrate, by passing a test of ten exercises, that they are all-around well-trained and well-behaved dogs. Agility trials, which are actually obstacle courses for

The Toy Fox Terrier is very collectible! Given the breed's petite size and limited demands, owners tend to own more than one at a time.

dogs, are fun for dog and owner, and Toy Fox Terrier owners find their dogs particularly well suited for this type of competition.

The activities that an owner can share with his well-trained Toy Fox Terrier are limited only by the amount of time invested. Owners not inclined toward competitive events might find enjoyment in having their Toy Fox Terriers serve as assistance or therapy dogs. Assistance dogs are trained to help their owners in a multitude of daily tasks, such as letting hearing-impaired owners know if the phone is ringing or if someone is knocking at the door. They also learn to retrieve articles that their owners may have dropped and are unable to reach.

Therapy dogs are trained to comfort and assist the sick, the elderly and often the handicapped by making visits to hospitals, orphanages and homes for the aged. It has been proven that these visits provide great therapeutic value to patients.

SPACE SAVER

The Toy Fox Terrier is probably one of the most economical dogs to own. He requires little space and quite frankly would prefer to share your bed rather than have you invest in his own dog bed. The Toy Fox eats little, probably less than other breeds of the same size. He can get all of the exercise he needs in a tiny yard or even within the confines of an apartment.

TOY FOX TERRIER

INTRODUCTION TO THE BREED STANDARD

In the earliest days of man's relationship with dogs, he began to see that those particular dogs constructed in a certain way were better suited to performing a particular task. Particular characteristics were prized and breeding practices were employed to perpetuate these characteristics.

The people who kept these dogs gathered to make comparisons and seek out stock to improve their own lines. The more successful keepers were asked to observe the dogs at work and evaluate them.

With urbanization, fewer and fewer dogs were given the opportunity to perform their intended functions. To avoid the respective breeds' losing their ability to perform, the fanciers began to select their stock based on the conformation that they determined would produce the most successful workers. The guidelines or "standards" became theoretical rather than practical.

Previously, the accent had been on function; now it was on form. It should be easy to see, once form was the keynote, how breeds whose only purpose was to be esthetically pleasing would gain an equal place of respect alongside their working-breed counterparts.

It should be noted here that these early breed descriptions were the forerunners of breed standards and that they were written by knowledgeable individuals in each breed for their peers. These experts were all thoroughly familiar with their respective breeds. Their descriptions were used primarily as checklists or blueprints to breed by, and they served as reminders so that important and defining points of the breed's conformation and character would not be lost.

Today's standards describe the ideal specimen of a breed. They are written by individuals versed in breed type and canine anatomy. They include descriptions of structure, temperament, coat, color and the manner in which the dog moves. The standards are used by breeders to assist them in breeding toward this goal of perfection. While no dog is absolutely perfect, the dogs that adhere closest to the ideal are what breeders will determine to be show or breeding stock. The dogs that deviate too far from the ideal are considered as companion or pet stock.

The standard is also used by dog-show judges to compare actual dogs to the ideal. The dog that the judge feels adheres closest to the ideal is the winner of the class, and so on down the line as the classes progress to Best in Show. First let's look at the United Kennel Club (UKC) standard and then we'll present the American Kennel Club's equivalent.

THE UNITED KENNEL CLUB BREED STANDARD FOR THE TOY FOX TERRIER
Revised January 1, 1999

HISTORY
The immediate ancestor of the Toy Fox Terrier is the larger Smooth Fox Terrier. The original Fox Terrier breed standard was written in England in 1876. The size of the breed at that time was 18 to 20 pounds. Owners of these brave little dogs found that the smallest, which they called "runts," were the scrappiest of the bunch. These little dogs were prized for their temperament. Smaller dogs were developed and eventually were found in the seven-pound range.

The United Kennel Club began registering the Smooth Fox Terrier in 1912. Between then and the mid-1920s, the Toy Fox Terrier was developed, being a miniature of the previous breed, however they were still registered under the name of

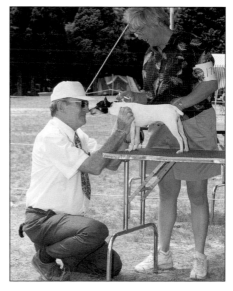

The standard describes the breed's correct body structure as well as the desired temperament, which should be friendly and eager to please, as this Toy Fox demonstrates to the judge!

Fox Terrier (Smooth). Those dogs appear almost identical to the dogs of today. It was not until February 24, 1936 that UKC began registering the Toy Fox Terrier under its current name.

GENERAL APPEARANCE
The Toy Fox Terrier is small in size, with a body that is square when viewed from the side. The length of the head, neck and legs are in proportion to the length and depth of the body. The body is compact, with the short tail carried upright. With a short, glossy coat that is predominantly white, the appearance is elegant, balanced and aristocratic. Highly intelligent, alert, loyal, fearless and having much endurance, this small dog, above all, has the conformation, characteristics and personality of a terrier.

The breed's outline should appear square with a compact body, short coat and short tail carried upright.

CHARACTERISTICS

The Toy Fox Terrier is self-possessed, spirited and determined. They are energetic, lively and strong for their size. They are not easily intimidated by other pets. Most are comical, entertaining and playful all of their life, which is generally long in comparison to many other breeds. They are friendly and loyal to their master or owners, yet protective. As a rule they are easily trained and adapt to showing in conformation and obedience. Any individuals lacking good terrier attitude and personality are to be faulted.

HEAD

A typical head unmistakably stamps the dog as being of this breed. The head is in proportion to the rest of the body. It resembles a blunt wedge when viewed from both the front and in profile. When viewed from the front, the head widens gradually from the black nose to the base of the ears in practically an unbroken line. The distance from the nose to the stop is equal to the distance from the stop to the occiput.

The skull is moderate in width and slightly rounded. The skull and muzzle are both in proportion to the length and overall size of the head. The muzzle tapers gradually from the base of the ears to the nose. Medium stop; somewhat sloping. The cheeks are flat and muscular, with the area below the eyes well filled-in. Close-lying lips.

Serious Faults: Domed skull (apple head). Flat skull. Deep, sharp stop. Shallow stop. Roman nose. *Faults:* Backskull or foreskull too wide. Narrow muzzle. Wide muzzle. Short muzzle. Long muzzle. Cheeks too bulgy or too flat.

Teeth: A full complement of strong, white teeth meeting in a scissors bite is preferred. An even bite is permissible. Loss of teeth should not be faulted for a dog of any age as long as the bite can be determined as correct. *Faults:* Overshot over 1/16 inch. Puppy teeth retained after one year of age.

Eyes: Dark in color; as dark as possible being preferred. Clear and bright, with a soft, intelligent expression. Globular, round, and somewhat prominent, yet not bulging. They are set well apart and fit well into the sockets. *Faults:* Light color. Too large or too small.

Protruding. Squinty. Dull. Set too wide apart. Set too close together. Lack of expression.

Nose: The nose is black in color. Puppies are usually born with pink-colored noses, which generally turn dark before or by weaning time. *Faults:* Brown nose. Brownish tinge. Small pink or flesh-colored specks on nose.

Ears: Pointed, inverted, V-shaped: placed well up on the sides of the head. Close together, but never touching. The inner base is on a level with the top of the skull. Always erect when alert; carried erect in motion. The size is in proportion to the size of the head and the overall size of the dog. *Serious Faults:* Rounded. Set too wide apart. Low-set. Too large. Too small. Flop ears.

NECK

The length of the neck is approximately the same as that of the head and is in proportion to the body and size of the dog. The neck widens gradually, blending smoothly into the shoulders. The neck is clean and is slightly arched in a graceful curve. *Faults:* Neck too short, too thick or with loose, excess skin. Ewe neck. Goose neck.

FOREQUARTERS

The shoulders are sloping and well-laid-back (approximately at a 45 degree angle); blending smoothly from neck to back.

Forelegs: When viewed from the side, the forelegs are straight from the elbows to the feet, which point forward. When viewed from the front, the forelegs are some distance apart and drop straight from the elbows to the feet. The elbows are close and perpendicular to the body. The pasterns are strong and straight while remaining flexible. Bone size is in proportion to the size of the dog. Dewclaw removal is optional, but recommended.

Faults: Straight shoulders. Loaded shoulders. Steep shoulders. Down in withers. Too far apart at withers. Out at elbows. Tied in elbows. Down in pasterns. Bowed front.

BODY

In shape, the body appears square when viewed from the side, with height approximately equal to length. The height is measured from the highest point of the withers to the bottom of the front feet. The

A Toy Fox Terrier of correct type, substance, structure and balance in profile.

A Toy Fox Terrier head study showing a dog with correct markings, structure, type and proportion.

bound. Barrel-chested. Narrow chest. Brisket too shallow or too deep. Pointed brisket (when viewed from front.)

HINDQUARTERS

Strong and muscular; free of droop or crouch. The rump is well-filled-in on each side of the tail. The hipbones are on a level with or just below the back. Good width and depth at pelvis. Good muscling over hips, blending smoothly down over the upper to the lower thighs. Any male six months of age, or older, should have two normal size testicles clearly visible and well-seated in the scrotum.

Hind legs: The hind legs appear strong and straight down to the feet. The upper and lower thighs are strong, well-muscled and of good

length is measured from the prosternum (front point of the shoulder - forechest) to the point of the buttocks. The body is balanced and tapers slightly from the ribs to the flank, with an evident, moderate tuck-up.

1 & 2: Dogs showing solid color without (1) and with (2) blaze, with ears and eyes fully marked. Both are correct. 3 & 4: A split faced dog (3) is incorrect. The ears being predominantly white with heavy ticking (4) is also incorrect.

The back is short and strong. The backline is strong, straight and firm, blending smoothly from the neck and shoulder to the tail. The chest is deep, with an oval-shaped, well-sprung rib cage. The brisket extends to or just above the elbows. The chest is in proportion and in balance with the rest of the body.

Serious Faults: Sway back. Roach back. Sloping croup. Taller at hips than at withers. Taller at withers than at hips. Short-bodied. Long-bodied. Too much or too little tuckup. Lack of muscling. Muscle

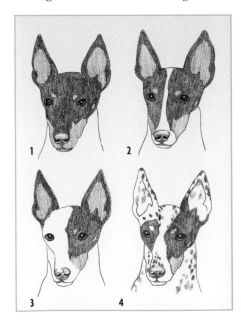

length. The stifles are clearly-
defined and well-angulated. The
hocks are well bent. When viewed
from the rear, the stifles, hocks and
feet are straight and parallel to each
other. Bone size is in proportion to
the size of the dog. If present,
dewclaws are removed.

Serious Faults: Sloping, break-
ing off in rump. Narrow and/or shallow pelvis. *Faults:* Hind legs lacking
angulation or over-angulated.
Hipbones above the back level. Lack
of muscle in hips and thighs. Too
much muscle in hips and thighs.
Thighs too short or too long. Bow-
hocked. Cowhocked. Straight in
stifle. Over-angulated stifle. Stifles
turning in or out. Legs too close
together or too far apart.

FEET
The feet are oval in shape and
compact, with arched toes and hard,
tough and well-cushioned pads.
Faults: Round feet. Splayed. Flat.
Feet turned in or out.

TAIL
Set on high and on a level with the
back. Carried gaily, above the hori-
zontal line of the back when the dog
is in motion or at attention; may be
dropped when the dog is at ease.
Docked with approximately 2/5th of
the full tail remaining; equivalent
length if a bobtail. Minimum length
about one inch, maximum length
about three inches, for dogs six
months of age or older. *Serious
Faults:* Tail curled. Tail carried

Faults: Incorrect heavy body ticking, upright shoulders, roached back, weak rear, cow-hocked and steep in croup.

Faults: Ewe neck, loaded shoulders, wide front with toeing out, low tail set, weak rear and steep in croup.

straight over the back. Set too low.
Faults: Too short. Too long. Not
carried gaily when in motion.

COAT
A distinguishing feature of the
breed, the coat is short, satiny and
shiny; fine in texture and smooth to
the touch. It is slightly longer at the
ruff (back of neck and shoulder);
uniformly covering the body. The

underline, inside of front legs, and lower part of back legs are covered with at least a thin coat of hair. The skin is firm but pliable. *Serious Fault:* Wiry coat. *Faults:* Too long, too coarse. Dry and dull. Too thin. Loose or non-pliable skin.

COLOR

White is the predominating body color. White is not the predominating head color. Predominating to mean "more than half".

Acceptable Colors and Color Patterns:

White and Black with Tan Trim: Black predominates on the head. The ears are black on the back with a very narrow, black rim on the inner edge. The tan trim is found on the cheeks and/or chops and as eye dots. Face with or without a white blaze. A blaze may extend onto either or both sides of the lower muzzle. White frost or tiny white spots on the lower muzzle are acceptable. White is the predominating body color, with or without black spots. Ticking is permitted to some degree provided the white predominates and general good looks are maintained. It is preferred that the black markings be free of any tan or brown shadings or very small tan or brown spots, but not faulted.

White and Black: Everything in regard to color and markings are the same as above, except there is no tan trim.

White and Tan: Tan predominates on the head. The ears are tan on the back with a very narrow tan rim on the inner edge. Trim is a lighter or darker shade of tan on the cheeks and/or chops and eye dots, if visible. Face with or without a white blaze. The blaze may extend onto either or both sides of the lower muzzle. White frost or tiny white spots on the lower muzzle are acceptable. The body is predominantly white, with or without tan spots. Ticking is permitted to some degree provided the white predominates and general good looks are maintained. It is preferred that the tan markings be free of any black or brown shadings or very small black

Faults: Excessive body markings (more than 50%), long backed, low tail set, straight in rear and upright shoulders.

Faults: Short neck, upright loaded shoulders, gay tail, straight in rear, shallow chest and lacking tuck-up.

or brown spots, but not faulted.

Faults: A wide blaze that extends up to the eyes. Black or tan coloring, other than speckling (ticking) on the legs below the wrist joint of the forelegs or the hock joint of the hind legs. Any variation from that which is stated for the color and markings in any color combination is a fault. In a White and Tan— tan markings that are too red, chocolate- shaded or brindled.

WEIGHT
Dogs six months of age or older must weigh from three-and-one-half up to, and including, seven pounds.

GAIT
Movement is smooth and flowing, with the legs moving straight, parallel and in a line at a walk or slow trot, with the back straight and the head and tail up. There is balance and coordination with good reach in the front and good drive from the rear. Movement is used to evaluate gait and to evaluate the parts involved in gait, therefore the points allotted to movement are included when considering all the dog's structural parts involved. In gaiting, the stifles, hocks and feet should turn neither in nor out, and the hind legs should move in line with the front legs. *Serious Fault:* Hackney gait.

DISQUALIFICATIONS
Unilateral or bilateral cryptorchid. Extreme viciousness or shyness.

Undershot bite. Overshot bite of more than 1/8 inch. Wry mouth. Liver colored nose. Dudley nose. No tail. Dogs of any age over seven pounds. Any dog six months of age or older weighing less than three-and-one-half pounds. Ears not erect on any dog over six months of age. Any solid-colored dog. Maltese or chocolate markings. Any color combination in which white is not the predominant body color. Any color combination other than stated combinations. In any color combination, any dog whose head is more than half white. Any dog whose head and/or ear color and body spots are of different colors.

SCALE OF POINTS

Head	20
Neck	5
Shoulders	10
Chest, Ribs, Underline (tuck up)	10
Back and Loin	10
Hindquarters (hips, croup, pelvis and thighs)	10
Tail (set and carriage)	5
Forelegs and Hind legs	10
Coat and Color	10
Characteristics, Attitude and Temperament	10
(anything else to complete the 'total' dog)	
TOTAL	**100**

THE AMERICAN KENNEL CLUB STANDARD FOR THE TOY FOX TERRIER

History: The Toy Fox Terrier is a true American breed developed by breeding small Smooth Fox Terriers with several toy breeds including the Chihuahua and Manchester Terrier. Today, the Toy Fox Terrier is a well-balanced toy dog of athletic appearance, displaying grace and agility in equal measure with strength and stamina. From the hunt to the show ring, the Toy Fox Terrier has become a cherished companion dog and excellent show piece. The Toy Fox Terrier has shown that he is at home in conformation, obedience and agility trials, his favorite spotlight is the center stage of his owner's life.

The Toy Fox Terrier is a toy and a terrier, and both have influenced his personality and character. While retaining the terrier gameness, courage and animation, the crossbreeding with various toy breeds mentioned created a milder disposition. Although easier to live with than many terriers, the Toy Fox Terrier is still a working terrier, and many of them delight in hunting and going to ground. Given the opportunity, the Toy Fox Terrier will pursue the quarry of the backyard or barnyard with diligence. Known to tree squirrels and flush out rodents, the hunt is always welcome. Flyball or fetch are easily learned and perfected for endless hours of activity. However, if you enjoy a lap dog, this little companion appears to know the latest in television entertainment of his household. Children especially enjoy the unending energy and zeal for play throughout this dog's life.

General Appearance: The Toy Fox Terrier is truly a toy and a terrier and both have influenced his personality and character. As a terrier, the Toy Fox Terrier possesses keen intelligence, courage, and animation. As a toy he is diminutive and devoted with an endless abiding love for his master. The Toy Fox Terrier is a well-balanced toy dog of athletic appearance displaying grace and agility in equal measure with strength and stamina. His lithe muscular body has a smooth elegant outline which conveys the impression of effortless movement and endless endurance. He is naturally well groomed, proud, animated and alert. Characteristic traits are his elegant head, his short glossy and predominantly white coat, coupled with a predominantly solid head, and his short high-set tail.

Size, Proportion and Substance: Size: 8.5–11.5 inches, 9–11 preferred, 8.5–11.5 acceptable. Proportion: The Toy Fox Terrier is square in proportion, with height being approximately equal to length; with height measured from withers to ground and length measured from point of shoulder to buttocks.

Slightly longer in bitches is acceptable. Substance: Bone must be strong, but not excessive and always in proportion to size. Overall balance is important. *Disqualification:* Any dog under 8.5 inches and over 11.5 inches.

Head: The head is elegant, balanced and expressive with no indication of coarseness. Expression is intelligent, alert, eager and full of interest. Eyes: Clear, bright and dark, including eye-rims, with the exception of chocolates whose eye-rims should be self-colored. The eyes are full, round and somewhat prominent, yet never bulging, with a soft intelligent expression. They are set well apart, not slanted, and fit well together into the sockets. Ears: The ears are erect, pointed, inverted V-shaped, set high and close together, but never touching. The size is in proportion to the head and body. *Disqualification:* Ears not erect on any dog over six months of age. Skull: Moderate in width, slightly rounded and softly wedge shaped. Medium stop, somewhat sloping. When viewed from the front, the head widens gradually from the nose to the base of the ears. The distance from the nose to the stop is equal to the distance from the stop to the occiput. The cheeks are flat and muscular, with the area below the eyes well filled in. *Faults:* Apple head. Muzzle: Strong rather than fine, in proportion to the head as a whole and parallel to the top of the

The desired forequarters should be well angulated, with shoulders firmly set, sloping and well laid back. Color extending beyond the dog's elbow is considered a fault.

skull. Nose: Black only with the exception of self-colored in chocolate dogs. *Disqualification:* Dudley nose. Lips: Small and tight fitting. Bite: A full complement of strong white teeth meeting in a scissors bite is preferred. Loss of teeth should not be faulted as long as the bite can be determined as correct. *Disqualification:* Undershot, wry mouth, overshot more than one-eighth inch.

Neck, Topline and Body: The neck is carried proudly erect, well set on, slightly arched, gracefully curved, clean, muscular and free from throatiness. It is proportioned to the head and body and widens gradually blending smoothly into the shoulders. The length of the neck is approximately the same as that of the head. The topline is level when standing and gaiting. The body is balanced and tapers slightly from ribs to flank. The chest is deep and muscular with well sprung ribs. Depth of chest extends to the point of elbow. The back is straight, level, and muscular. Short and strong in loin with moderate tuck-up to denote grace and elegance. The croup is level with topline and well-rounded. The tail is set high, held erect and in proportion to the size of the dog. Docked to the third or fourth joint.

Forequarters: Forequarters are well angulated. The shoulder is firmly set and has adequate muscle, but is not overdeveloped. The shoulders are sloping and well laid back, blending smoothly from neck to back. The forechest is well developed. The elbows are close and perpendicular to the body. The legs are parallel and straight to the pasterns which

are strong and straight while remaining flexible. Feet are small and oval, pointing forward turning neither in nor out. Toes are strong, well-arched and closely knit with deep pads.

Hindquarters: Hindquarters are well angulated, strong and muscular. The upper and lower thighs are strong, well muscled and of good length. The stifles are clearly defined and well angulated. Hock joints are well let down and firm. The rear pasterns are straight. The legs are parallel from the rear and turn neither in nor out. Dewclaws should be removed from hindquarters if present.

Coat: The coat is shiny, satiny, fine in texture and smooth to the touch. It is slightly longer in the ruff, uniformly covering the body.

Color: Tri-color: Predominately black head with sharply defined tan markings on cheeks, lips and eye dots. Body is over 50% white, with or without black body spots. White, Chocolate and Tan: Predominately chocolate head with sharply defined tan markings on cheeks, lips and eye dots. Body is over 50% white, with or without chocolate body spots. White and Tan: Predominately tan head. Body is over 50% white, with or without tan body spots. White and Black: Predominately black head. Body is over 50% white with or without black body spots. Color should be

MEETING THE IDEAL
The American Kennel Club defines a standard as: "A description of the ideal dog of each recognized breed, to serve as an ideal against which dogs are judged at shows." This "blueprint" is drawn up by the breed's recognized parent club, approved by a majority of its membership, and then submitted to the AKC for approval. This is a complete departure from the way standards are handled in England, where all standards and changes are controlled by The Kennel Club.

rich and clear. Blazes are acceptable, but may not touch the eyes or ears. Clear white is preferred, but a small amount of ticking is not to be penalized. *Faults:* Color, other than ticking, that extends below the elbow or the hock. *Disqualifications:* A blaze extending into the eyes or ears. Any color combination not stated above. Any dog whose head is more than 50% white. Any dog whose body is not more than 50% white. Any dog whose head and body spots are of different colors.

Gait: Movement is smooth and flowing with good reach and strong drive. The topline should remain straight and head and tail carriage erect while gaiting. *Fault:* Hackney gait.

Temperament: The Toy Fox Terrier is intelligent, alert and friendly, and loyal to his owners. He learns new tasks quickly, is eager to please, and adapts to almost any situation. The Toy Fox Terrier, like other terriers, is self-possessed, spirited, determined and not easily intimidated. He is a highly animated toy dog that is comical, entertaining and playful all of his life. Any individuals lacking good terrier attitude and personality are to be faulted.

Disqualifications
Any dog under 8.5 inches or over 11.5 inches.
Ears not erect on any dog over six months of age.

The hindquarters are strong, well angulated, with clearly defined stifles and firm hock joints, well let down. From the rear, the legs are straight and parallel.

Dudley nose.
Undershot, wry mouth, overshot more than one-eighth inch.
A blaze extending into the eye or ears.
Any color combination not stated above.
Any dog whose head is more than 50% white.
Any dog whose body is not more than 50% white.
Any dog whose head and body are of different colors.

Approved: July 11, 2000
Effective: April 1, 2001

TOY FOX TERRIER

WHERE TO BEGIN

If, after learning about the breed, you are convinced that the Toy Fox Terrier is in fact the ideal dog for you, it's time to learn about where to find a puppy and what to look for. Locating a breeder of Toy Fox Terriers should not present too much of a problem for the new owner, as this is a breed that's steadily gaining in popularity. You should inquire about breeders who enjoy a good reputation in the breed. You are looking for an established breeder with outstanding dog ethics and a strong

Good breeders will have their young puppies examined by a vet before it's time for the pups to leave for new homes, and will have the necessary health documentation to give the new owner.

> **PUPPY APPEARANCE**
> Your puppy should have a well-fed appearance but not a distended abdomen, which may indicate worms or incorrect feeding, or both. The body should be firm, with a solid feel. The skin of the abdomen should be pale pink and clean, without signs of scratching or rash. Check the hind legs to make certain that dewclaws were removed, if any were present at birth.

commitment to the breed.

New owners should have as many questions as they have doubts. An established breeder is indeed the one to answer your four million questions and make you comfortable with your choice of the Toy Fox Terrier. An established breeder will sell you a puppy at a fair price if, and only if, the breeder determines that you are a suitable, worthy owner of his dogs. An established breeder can be relied upon for advice, no matter what time of day or night. A reputable breeder will accept a puppy back, without questions, should you decide that this is not the right dog for you.

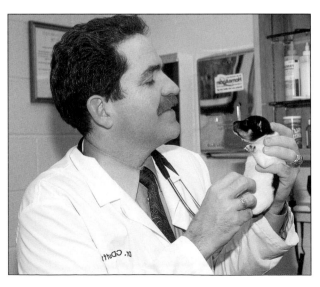

When choosing a breeder, reputation is much more important than convenience of location. Do not be overly impressed by breeders who run brag advertisements in the dog presses about their stupendous champions. The real quality breeders are quiet and unassuming. You hear about them at dog shows and trials, by word of mouth.

You may be well advised to avoid the novice who lives only a few miles away. The novice breeder, trying so hard to get rid of that first litter of puppies, is more than accommodating and anxious to sell you one. That breeder will charge you as much as any established breeder. The novice breeder isn't going to interrogate you and your family about your intentions with the puppy, the environment and training you can provide, etc. That breeder will be nowhere to be found when your poorly bred, badly adjusted four-pawed monster starts to growl and spit up at midnight or eat the family cat!

Choosing a breeder is an important first step in dog ownership. Fortunately, the majority of Toy Fox Terrier breeders is devoted to the breed and its well-being. New owners should have little problem finding a reputable breeder who doesn't live on the other side of the state (or in a different state). The American Kennel Club is able to refer you to

TEMPERAMENT COUNTS
Your selection of a good puppy can be determined by your needs. A show potential or a good pet? It is your choice. Every puppy, however, should be of good temperament. Although show-quality puppies are bred and raised with emphasis on physical conformation, responsible breeders strive for equally good temperament. Do not buy from a breeder who concentrates solely on physical beauty at the expense of personality.

breeders of quality Toy Fox Terriers, as can an all-breed club or a Toy Fox Terrier breed club, such as the American Toy Fox Terrier Club.

Potential owners are encouraged to attend dog shows and trials to see the Toy Fox Terriers in action, to meet the owners and

ARE YOU A FIT OWNER?

If the breeder from whom you are buying a puppy asks you a lot of personal questions, do not be insulted. Such a breeder wants to be sure that you will be a fit provider for his puppy.

handlers firsthand and to get an idea of what Toy Fox Terriers look like outside a photographer's lens. Provided you approach the handlers when they are not busy with the dogs, most are more than willing to answer questions, recommend breeders and give advice.

Once you have contacted and met a breeder or two and made your choice about which breeder is best suited to your needs, it's time to visit the litter. Litter size varies greatly in the breed. Usually there are two or three puppies in a litter, but litters of four, five and even six puppies are not entirely out of the ordinary.

Keep in mind that many top breeders have waiting lists. Sometimes new owners have to wait over a year for a puppy, especially if seeking a show- or breeding-quality Toy Fox Terrier. If you are really committed to the breeder whom you've selected, then you will wait (and hope for an early arrival!). If not, you may have to go with your second- or third-choice breeder. Don't be too anxious, however. If the breeder doesn't have a waiting list, or anyone interested in his pups, there is probably a good reason. It's no different than visiting a restaurant with no clientele. The best restaurants always have waiting lists—and it's usually worth the wait. Besides, isn't a puppy more important than a fancy dinner?

Since you are likely to be choosing a Toy Fox Terrier as a pet dog and not a show dog, you simply should select a pup that is friendly, attractive and healthy. If you have a preference for a male or female puppy, this will play a role in your selection as well. It can honestly be said that both the male and the female Toy Fox Terrier make wonderful companions. Females may be slightly more independent.

Breeders commonly allow visitors to see their litters by around the fifth or sixth week, and puppies leave for their new

Feisty, outgoing puppies make themselves known in the litter. Interaction between littermates helps the puppies learn just how hard they can bite without hurting their playmates.

homes between the eighth and tenth week (although sometimes show-quality pups are kept a few weeks longer so that the breeder can better evaluate their potential). Breeders who permit their puppies to leave early are more interested in a profit than in their puppies' well-being. Puppies need to learn the rules of the pack from their dam, and most dams continue teaching the pups manners and dos and don'ts until

around the eighth week. Due to the Toy Fox pups' small size at eight weeks old, the breeder should provide you with special instructions about handling, feeding, naps, etc.

During the pups' time with their breeder, the breeder will spend significant amounts of time with the Toy Fox toddlers so that the pups are able to interact with the "other species," i.e., humans. Given the long history that dogs and humans have, bonding between the two species is natural but must be nurtured. A well-bred, well-socialized Toy Fox Terrier pup wants nothing more than to be near you and please you.

Puppies and children should be introduced with caution and supervision. Toddlers never should be alone with or allowed to handle a Toy Fox puppy.

ARE YOU PREPARED?

Unfortunately, when a puppy is bought by someone who does not take into consideration the time and attention that dog ownership requires, it is the puppy who suffers when he is either abandoned or placed in a shelter by a frustrated owner. So all of the "homework" you do in preparation for your pup's arrival will benefit you both. The more informed you are, the more you will know what to expect and the better equipped you will be to handle the ups and downs of raising a puppy. Hopefully, everyone in the household is willing to do his part in raising and caring for the pup. The anticipation of owning a dog often brings a lot of promises from excited family members: "I will walk him every day," "I will feed him," "I will house-train him," etc., but these things take time and effort, and promises can easily be forgotten once the novelty of the new pet has worn off.

RECOGNIZING A SOUND AND HEALTHY PUPPY

The Toy Fox Terrier puppy you bring into your home will be your best friend and a member of your family for many years to come.

Well-bred and well-cared-for Toy Fox Terriers can easily live to be 10, 12, even 13 years of age. Therefore, it is of the utmost importance that the puppy you select has had every opportunity to begin life in a healthy, stable environment and comes from stock that is both physically and temperamentally sound.

The only way you can be assured of this is to go directly to a breeder of Toy Fox Terriers who has consistently produced dogs of this kind over the years. A breeder earns this reputation through a well-planned breeding program that has been governed by rigid selectivity. Selective breeding programs are aimed at maintaining the breed's many fine qualities and keeping the breed free of as many genetic weaknesses as possible.

Not all good breeders maintain large kennels. In fact, you are more apt to find that Toy Fox Terriers come from the homes of small hobby breeders who keep

Your chosen puppy should be alert and active, ready to play or investigate his surroundings.

PEDIGREE VS. REGISTRATION CERTIFICATE

Too often new owners are confused between these two important documents. Your puppy's pedigree, essentially a family tree, is a written record of a dog's genealogy of three generations or more. The pedigree will show you the names as well as performance titles of all of the dogs in your pup's background. Your breeder must provide you with a registration application, with his part properly filled out. You must complete the application and send it to the AKC or UKC with the proper fee. Every puppy must come from a litter that has been registered by the breeder, born in the US and from a sire and dam that are also registered with the AKC or UKC.

The seller must provide you with complete records to identify the puppy. The registry requires that the seller provide the buyer with the following: breed; sex, color and markings; date of birth; litter number (when available); names and registration numbers of the parents; breeder's name; and date sold or delivered.

just a few dogs and have litters only occasionally. The names of these people are just as likely to appear on the recommended lists from kennel clubs as the larger kennels that maintain many dogs.

Dedicated hobby breeders are equally devoted to breeding quality

Toy Fox Terriers. A factor in favor of the hobby breeder is the distinct advantage of their being able to raise their puppies in the home environment with all of the accompanying personal attention and socialization.

A healthy Toy Fox Terrier puppy is a bouncy, playful extrovert. Never select a puppy that appears shy or listless because you feel sorry for the pup. Doing so will undoubtedly lead to heartache and expensive veterinary costs. Do not attempt to make up for what the breeder did not do in providing proper care and nutrition. It seldom works.

Ask the breeder if it is possible take the puppy to which you are attracted (or the one that is attracted to you) into a different room in the kennel or house in which the pup was raised. The smells will remain the same for the puppy, so he should still feel secure, and this will give you an opportunity to see how the puppy acts away from his littermates and to inspect the puppy more closely.

Even though Toy Fox Terrier puppies are very small, they should feel sturdy to the touch. Puppies should not feel bony nor should their abdomens be bloated and extended. A puppy that has just eaten may have a little belly that is full, but the puppy should never appear obese.

The inside of a healthy puppy's ears will be pink and

TIME TO GO HOME
Breeders rarely release puppies until they are eight to ten weeks of age. This is an acceptable age for most breeds of dog, although some toy breeds are not released until around 12 weeks of age. If a breeder has a puppy that is 12 weeks of age or older, he is likely well socialized and house-trained. Be sure that he is otherwise healthy before deciding to take him home.

clean. Dark discharge or a bad odor could indicate ear mites, a sure sign of lack of cleanliness and poor maintenance. A Toy Fox Terrier puppy's breath should always smell sweet. Teeth must be clean and bright, and there should never be a malformation of the jaw, lips or nostrils. The puppy's bite should be neither overshot nor undershot, although small faults may correct themselves as the puppy matures. Discuss this with the breeder to see what he predicts.

The puppy's eyes should be dark and clear. Runny eyes or eyes that appear red and irritated could be caused by a myriad of problems, none of which indicates a healthy puppy. Coughing and diarrhea are danger signals as well, as is any discharge from the nose or eruptions on the skin. The coat should be soft, clean and lustrous.

Sound conformation can be determined even at eight weeks of age. The puppy's legs should be straight without bumps or malformations. The toes should point straight ahead. The back should be strong and level.

The puppy's attitude tells you a great deal about his state of health. Puppies that are feeling "out of sorts" react very quickly.

All dogs, whether puppies or adults, need chew-worthy toys to play with. Soft toys are the choice of young dogs, though supervision with such toys is well advised.

PET INSURANCE

Just as you can insure your car, your house and your own health, you likewise can insure your dog's health. Investigate a pet insurance policy by talking to your vet. Depending on the age of your dog, the breed and the kind of coverage you desire, your policy can be very affordable. Most policies cover accidental injuries, poisoning and thousands of medical problems and illnesses, including cancers. Some carriers also offer routine care and immunization coverage.

They will usually find a warm littermate with whom to snuggle and prefer to stay that way, even when the rest of the "gang" wants to play or go exploring.

It is hard to give a firm and fast rule as to when a Toy Fox Terrier puppy's ears will be standing up properly. It varies from bloodline to bloodline and just as much from one puppy to the next. Some ears are up as early as when the puppies are toddling about; others can take as long as six months.

SELECTING A SHOW-POTENTIAL PUPPY

There are many "beauty-point" shortcomings that a Toy Fox Terrier puppy might have that would in no way interfere with his being a wonderful companion. However, these faults could be serious drawbacks in the show ring. Many of these things are such that a beginner in the breed might hardly notice. This is why employing the assistance of a good breeder is so important in making your selection.

All of the foregoing regarding soundnoss and health in selecting a companion puppy applies to the show-prospect puppy as well. The show prospect must also be sound and healthy, and must adhere to the standard of the breed very closely.

Like the pet, the show prospect must have a happy, outgoing temperament. He will be a compact little bundle of energy, never appearing short-legged or out of balance. The show puppy will move around with ease, his head held high. Dark eyes and black nose, lips and eye-rims are required except in the self-colors.

The younger a puppy is, the more unpredictable his future as a show dog will be. The most a good breeder will say about a very young puppy is that the puppy has show potential. The breeder's experience with and knowledge of the developmental stages of outstanding dogs that he has produced in the past will increase the predictability factor, but any experienced breeder will tell you that the closer a dog is to full maturity, the better he is able to evaluate the dog as a show dog.

HANDLE WITH CARE
You should be extremely careful about handling tiny puppies. Not that you might hurt them, but that the pups' mother may exhibit what is called "maternal aggression." It is a natural, instinctive reaction for the dam to protect her young against anything she interprets as predatory or possibly harmful to her pups. The sweetest, most gentle of bitches, after whelping a litter, often reacts this way, even to her owner.

COMMITMENT OF OWNERSHIP
After considering all of the foregoing factors, you have most likely already made some very important decisions about selecting your puppy. You have chosen the Toy Fox Terrier, which means that you have decided which characteristics you want in a dog and what type of dog will best fit into your family and lifestyle. If you

PUPPY PERSONALITY

When a litter becomes available to you, choosing a pup out of all those adorable faces will not be an easy task! Sound temperament is of utmost importance, but each pup has its own personality and some may be better suited to you than others. A feisty, independent pup will do well in a home with older children and adults, while quiet, shy puppies will thrive in a home with minimal noise and distractions. Your breeder knows the pups best and should be able to guide you in the right direction.

have selected a breeder, you have gone a step further—you have done your research and found a responsible, conscientious person who breeds quality Toy Fox Terriers and who should be a reliable source of help as you and your puppy adjust to life together. If you have observed a litter in action, you have obtained a first-hand look at the dynamics of a puppy "pack" and, thus, you have

learned about each pup's individual personality—perhaps you have even found one that particularly appeals to you.

However, even if you have not yet found the Toy Fox Terrier puppy of your dreams, observing pups will help you learn to recognize certain behavior and to determine what a pup's behavior indicates about his temperament. You will be able to pick out which pups are the leaders, which ones are less outgoing, which ones are confident, shy, playful, friendly, aggressive, etc. Equally as important, you will learn to recognize what a healthy pup should look and act like. All of these things will help you in your search, and when you find the Toy Fox Terrier that was meant for you, you will know it!

Researching your breed, selecting a responsible breeder and observing as many pups as possible are all important steps on the way to dog ownership. It may seem like a lot of effort…and you have not even taken the pup home yet! Remember, though, you cannot be too careful when it comes to deciding on the type of dog you want and finding out about your prospective pup's background. Buying a puppy is not—or *should* not be—just another whimsical purchase. This is one instance in which you actually do get to choose your own family!

You may be thinking that buying a puppy should be fun—it should not be so serious and so much work. Keep in mind that your puppy is not a cuddly stuffed toy or decorative lawn ornament; rather, he is a living creature that will become a real member of your family. You will come to realize that, while buying a puppy is a pleasurable and exciting endeavor, it is not something to be taken lightly. Relax...the fun will start when the pup comes home!

Always keep in mind that a puppy is nothing more than a baby in a furry disguise...a baby who is virtually helpless in a human world and who trusts his owner for fulfillment of his basic needs for survival. In addition to food, water and shelter, your pup needs care, protection, guidance and love. If you are not prepared to commit to this, then you are not prepared to own a dog.

"Wait a minute," you say. "How hard could this be? All of my neighbors own dogs and they seem to be doing just fine. Why should I have to worry about all of this?" Well, you should not worry about it; in fact, you will probably find that once your Toy Fox Terrier pup gets used to his new home, he will fall into his place in the family quite naturally. However, it never hurts to emphasize the commitment of dog ownership. With some time and patience, it is really not too difficult to raise a curious and exuberant Toy Fox Terrier pup to be a well-adjusted and well-mannered adult dog—a dog that could be your most loyal friend.

PREPARING PUPPY'S PLACE IN YOUR HOME

Researching your breed and finding a breeder are only two aspects of the "homework" you will have to do before taking your Toy Fox Terrier puppy home. You will also have to prepare your home and family for the new addition. Much as you would prepare a nursery

The breeder likely can introduce you to other family members (uncles, half-siblings, etc.) who will give you a good idea of how your chosen puppy will develop, both physically and temperamentally.

for a newborn baby, you will need to designate a place in your home that will be the puppy's own. How you prepare your home will depend on how much freedom the dog will be allowed. Whatever you decide, you must ensure that he has a place that he can "call his own."

Baby gates are an excellent purchase; these are the same gates that parents choose to keep their toddlers from wandering into certain areas of the home.

When you take your new puppy into your home, you are bringing him into what will become his home as well. Obviously, you did not buy a puppy with the intentions of catering to his every whim and allowing him to "rule the roost," but in order for a puppy to grow

"YOU BETTER SHOP AROUND!"
Finding a reputable breeder who sells healthy pups is very important, but make sure that the breeder you choose is not only someone you respect but also someone with whom you feel comfortable. Your breeder will be a resource long after you buy your puppy, and you must be able to call with reasonable questions without being made to feel like a pest! If you don't connect on a personal level, investigate some other breeders before making a final decision.

into a stable, well-adjusted dog, he has to feel comfortable in his surroundings. Remember, he is leaving the warmth and security of his mother and littermates, as well as the familiarity of the only place he has ever known, so it is important to make his transition as easy as possible.

By preparing a place in your home for the puppy, you are making him feel as welcome as possible in a strange new place. It should not take him long to get used to it, but the sudden shock of being transplanted is somewhat traumatic for a young pup. Imagine how a small child would feel in the same situation—that is how your puppy must be feeling. It is up to you to reassure him and to let him know, "Little one, you are going to like it here!"

WHAT YOU SHOULD BUY

CRATE

To someone unfamiliar with the use of crates in dog training, it may seem like punishment to shut a dog in a crate, but this is not the case at all. More and more breeders and trainers around the world are recommending crates as preferred tools for pet puppies as well as show puppies.

Crates are not cruel—crates have many humane and highly effective uses in dog care and training. For example, crate training is a popular and very successful housebreaking method. In addition, a crate can keep your dog safe during travel and, perhaps most importantly, a crate provides your dog with a place of his own in your home. It serves as a "doggie bedroom" of sorts—your Toy Fox Terrier can curl up in his crate when he wants to sleep or when he just needs a break. Many dogs sleep in their crates overnight. With soft bedding and his favorite toy, a crate becomes a cozy pseudo-den for your dog. Like his ancestors, he too will seek out the comfort and retreat of a den—you just happen to be providing him with something a little more luxurious than what his early ancestors enjoyed.

As far as purchasing a crate, the type that you buy is up to you. It will most likely be one of the two most popular types: wire or

YOUR SCHEDULE . . .
If you lead an erratic, unpredictable life, with daily or weekly changes in your work requirements, consider the problems of owning a puppy. The new puppy has to be fed regularly, socialized (loved, petted, handled, introduced to other people) and, most importantly, allowed to go outdoors for house-training. As the dog gets older, he can be more tolerant of deviations in his feeding and relief schedule.

fiberglass. There are advantages and disadvantages to each type. For example, a wire crate is more open, allowing the air to flow through and affording the dog a view of what is going on around him; these are preferred for use in the home. A fiberglass crate is sturdier and preferred as a travel crate. Although both types of crates can double as travel crates,

PHOTO COURTESY OF DOSKOCIL

Your local pet shop will have a wide variety of crates suitable for a Toy Fox Terrier. A small crate will be fine for the Toy Fox at his puppy and adult size.

this is easy since they do not grow to be very big. The Toy Fox puppy will not feel overwhelmed in a crate suitable for an adult Toy Fox. The recommended crate size is 21 inches (53.3 cm) deep by 16 inches (40.6 cm) wide by 15 inches (38.1 cm) high.

BEDDING

A soft crate pad and/or a blanket in the dog's crate will help the dog feel more at home. First, these will take the place of the leaves, twigs, etc., that the pup would use in the wild to make a den; the pup can make his own "burrow" in the crate. Although your pup is far removed from his den-making ancestors, the denning instinct is still a part of his genetic makeup. Second, until you take your pup home, he has been sleeping amid the warmth of his mother and littermates, and while soft bedding is not the same as a warm, breathing body, it still provides heat and something with which to snuggle. You will want to wash your pup's bedding frequently in case he has a potty "accident" in his crate, and replace or remove any item in the crate that becomes ragged and starts to fall apart.

providing protection for the dog, you may wish to purchase a wire crate for the home and a fiberglass crate for traveling. Fiberglass crates usually have handles on top for easy carrying.

When purchasing the crate, it is best to get one that will accommodate your dog both as a pup and at full size. With toy breeds,

TOYS

Toys are a must for dogs of all ages, especially for curious playful pups. Puppies are the "children" of the dog world, and what child does not love toys? Chew toys provide enjoyment for both dog and owner—your dog will enjoy playing with his favorite toys, while you will enjoy the fact that they distract him from chewing on your expensive shoes and leather sofa. Puppies love to chew; in fact, chewing is a physical need for pups as they are teething, and everything looks appetizing! The full range of your possessions—from old dish rag to Oriental carpet—are fair game in the eyes of a teething pup. Puppies are not all that discerning when it comes to finding something literally to "sink their teeth into"—everything tastes great!

Toy Fox Terriers enjoy passing the time away by chewing, and it seems that the more alpha-type members of the breed will be even more inclined to chew. Toy Fox Terriers need toys that do not destruct easily. Big, chunky rope toys and synthetically made shatter-proof bones are good choices.

Breeders advise owners to resist stuffed toys, because they can become de-stuffed in no time. The overly excited pup may ingest the stuffing, which is neither nutritious nor digestible. Similarly, squeaky toys are quite popular, but must be avoided for the Toy Fox Terrier. Perhaps a squeaky toy can be used as an aid in training or during playtime under your supervision, but not for free play. If a pup "disembow-

els" one of these, the small plastic squeaker inside can be dangerous if swallowed.

Be careful of natural bones, which have a tendency to splinter into sharp, dangerous pieces. Also be careful of rawhide, which can

CRATE-TRAINING TIPS

During crate training, you should partition off the section of the crate in which the pup stays. If he is given too big an area, this will hinder your training efforts. Crate training is based on the fact that a dog does not like to soil his sleeping quarters, so it is ineffective to keep a pup in an area that is so big that he can eliminate in one end and get far enough away from it to sleep. Also, you want to make the crate den-like for your dog. Blankets and a favorite toy will make the crate cozy for the small pup; as he grows, you may want to evict some of his "roommates" to make more room. It will take some coaxing at first, but be patient. Given some time to get used to it, your dog will adapt to his home-within-a-home quite nicely.

TOYS, TOYS, TOYS!

With a big variety of dog toys available, and so many that look like they would be a lot of fun for a dog, be careful in your selection. It is amazing what a set of puppy teeth can do to an innocent-looking toy, so, obviously, safety is a major consideration. Be sure to choose the most durable products that you can find. Hard nylon bones and toys are a safe bet, and many of them are offered in different scents and flavors that will be sure to capture your dog's attention. It is always fun to play a game of fetch with your dog, and there are balls and flying discs that are specially made to withstand dog teeth.

turn into pieces that are easy to swallow and become a mushy mess on your carpet.

It is important to only provide your Toy Fox with the safest toys available; remember, although a small dog, he has strong jaws and teeth. Monitor the condition of all your pup's toys carefully and get rid of any that have been chewed to the point of becoming potentially dangerous.

Leash

A nylon leash is probably the best option, as it is the most resistant to puppy teeth should your pup take a liking to chewing on his leash. Of course, this is a habit that should be nipped in the bud, but, if your pup likes to chew on his leash, he has a very slim chance of being able to chew through the strong nylon. Nylon leashes are also lightweight, which is good for a young Toy Fox Terrier who is just getting used to the idea of walking on a leash. For everyday walking and safety purposes, the nylon leash is a good choice.

As your pup grows up and gets used to walking on the leash, and can do it politely, you may want to purchase a flexible leash. These leashes allow you to extend the length to give the dog a broader area to explore or to shorten the length to keep the dog near you. Some owners of toy breeds like to use lightweight

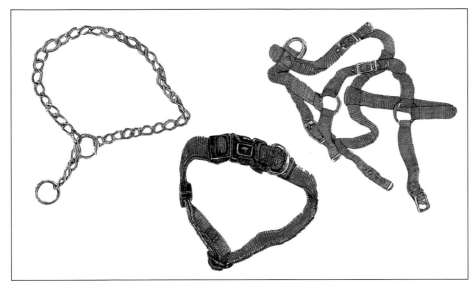

Your local pet shop will have a variety of collars, leashes and harnesses from which you can select those best suited to your Toy Fox Terrier.

harnesses on their dogs and feel that they are more comfortable for small dogs than the traditional leash and collar.

COLLAR

Your pup should get used to wearing a collar all the time since you will want to attach his ID tags to it; plus, you have to attach the leash to something! A lightweight nylon collar is a good choice. Make certain that the collar fits snugly enough so that the pup cannot wriggle out of it, but is loose enough so that it will not be uncomfortably tight around the pup's neck. You should be able to fit a finger between the pup's neck and the collar. It may take some time for your pup to get used to wearing the collar, but soon he will not

notice that it is there. Choke collars are made for training, but are neither recommended nor suitable for use with toy breeds.

FOOD AND WATER BOWLS

Your pup will need two bowls, one for food and one for water. You may also want an additional water bowl to keep outside for your dog. Stainless steel or sturdy plastic bowls are popular choices. Plastic bowls are more chewable, but dogs tend not to chew on the steel variety, which can be sterilized. It is important to buy sturdy bowls since anything is in danger of being chewed by puppy teeth and you do not want your dog to be constantly chewing apart his bowl (for his safety and for your wallet!).

Small bowls are sufficient for Toy Fox Terriers. Purchase bowls that are durable and can be cleaned easily.

PHOTO COURTESY OF MIKKI PET PRODUCTS

CLEANING SUPPLIES

Until a pup is housebroken, you will be doing a lot of cleaning. "Accidents" will occur, which is acceptable in the beginning stages of toilet training because the puppy does not know any better. All you can do is be prepared to clean up any accidents as soon as they happen. Old rags or towels, paper towels, newspapers and a safe disinfectant are good to have on hand.

BEYOND THE BASICS

The items previously discussed are the bare necessities. You will find out what else you need as you go along—grooming supplies, flea/tick protection, baby gates to partition a room, etc. These things will vary depending on your situation, but it is important that right away you have everything you need to feed and make your Toy Fox Terrier comfortable in his first few days at home.

PUPPY-PROOFING YOUR HOME

Aside from making sure that your Toy Fox Terrier will be comfortable in your home, you also have to make sure that your home is safe for your Toy Fox Terrier. This means taking precautions that your pup will not get into anything he should not get into and that there is nothing within his reach that may harm him should he sniff it, chew it, inspect it, etc. This probably seems obvious since, while you are primarily concerned with your pup's safety, at the same time you do not want your belongings to be ruined. Breakables should be placed out of reach if your dog is to have full run of the house. If he is to be limited to certain places within the house, keep any potentially dangerous items in the "off-limits" areas.

An electrical cord can pose a danger should the puppy decide to taste it—and who is going to convince a pup that it would not make a great chew toy? Wires and cords should be fastened tightly against the wall and away from puppy teeth. If your dog is going to spend time in a crate, make sure that there is nothing near his crate that he can reach if he sticks his curious little nose or paws through the openings. Just as you would with a child, keep all household cleaners and chemicals where the pup cannot reach them; antifreeze is especially dangerous

It is your responsibility to clean up after your Toy Fox Terrier relieves himself. Pet shops have various aids to make the cleanup task less of a chore.

to dogs, as they seem to be attracted to its taste and it causes death quickly.

It is also important to make sure that the outside of your home is safe. Of course, your puppy should never be unsupervised, but a pup let loose in the fenced yard will want to run and explore, and he should be granted that freedom. Do not let a fence give you a false sense of security; you would be surprised at how crafty (and persistent) a dog can be in figuring out how to dig under and squeeze his way through small holes, or to jump or climb over a fence. Toy Fox Terriers are excellent jumpers and love to dig. They are easily

NATURAL TOXINS

Examine your grass and landscaping before bringing your puppy home. Many varieties of plants have leaves, stems or flowers that are toxic if ingested, and you can depend on a curious puppy to investigate them. Ask your vet for information on poisonous plants or research them at your library.

Your vet will become your Toy Fox's best friend (next to you, of course!) throughout the dog's life.

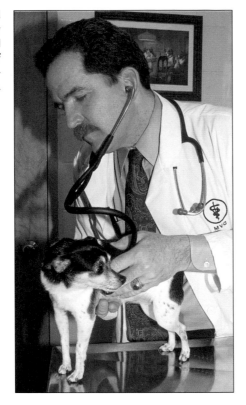

gaps in the fence. Keep a close eye on any spots in which you've noticed your Toy Fox digging or trying to get over, since a very determined pup may return to the same spot to "work on it."

FIRST TRIP TO THE VET

You have selected your puppy, and your home and family are ready. Now all you have to do is collect your Toy Fox Terrier from the breeder and the fun begins, right? Well...not so fast. Something else you need to plan is your pup's first trip to the veterinarian. Perhaps the breeder can recommend someone in the area who specializes in terriers or small breeds, or maybe you know some other Toy Fox Terrier owners who can suggest a good vet. Either way, you should have an appointment arranged for your pup before you pick him up.

Be certain that your lawn is safe for your Toy Fox Terrier. Many common fertilizers and weed killers can be harmful to dogs.

capable of jumping as high as 3 feet straight in the air from a stand-still position. They climb as well. An absolute minimum for fencing would be 3 feet, but a height of at least 4 feet is highly recommended for outdoor fencing.

Because of the breed's propensity and aptitude for digging, it is equally important to make the fence well embedded into the ground (at least a foot deep). Check the fence periodically to ensure that it is in good shape and be sure to repair or secure any

The pup's first visit will consist of an overall examination to make sure that the pup does not have any problems that are not apparent to you. The veterinarian will also set up a schedule for the pup's vaccinations; the breeder will inform you of which ones the pup has already received and the vet can continue from there.

INTRODUCTION TO THE FAMILY

Everyone in the house will be excited about the puppy's coming home and will want to pet him and play with him, but it is best to make the introduction low-key so as not to overwhelm the puppy. He is apprehensive already. It is the first time he has been separated from his mother and the breeder, and the ride to your home is likely to be the first time he has been in a car. The last thing you want to do is smother him, as this will only frighten him further. This is not to say that human contact is not extremely necessary at this stage, because this is the time when a connection between the pup and his human family is formed. Gentle petting and soothing words should help console him, as well as just putting him down and letting him explore on his own (under your watchful eye, of course).

The pup may approach the family members or may busy

himself with exploring for a while. Gradually, each person should spend some time with the pup, one at a time, crouching down to get as close to the pup's level as possible, letting him sniff each person's hands and petting him gently. He definitely needs human attention and he needs to be touched—this is how to form an immediate bond. Just remember that the pup is experiencing

Alert, intelligent and adaptable, your Toy Fox Terrier will grow from a bundle of puppy exuberance into an enjoyable companion with whom you can share many activities.

Soft warm bedding keeps the pup cozy and helps him feel comfortable.

many things for the first time, at the same time. There are new people, new noises, new smells and new things to investigate, so be gentle, be affectionate and be as comforting as you can be.

PUP'S FIRST NIGHT HOME
You have traveled home with your new charge safely in his crate. He's been to the vet for a thorough check-up; he's been weighed, his papers have been examined and perhaps he's even been vaccinated and wormed as well. He's met (and licked!) the whole family, including the excited children and the less-than-happy cat. He's explored his area, his new bed, the yard and anywhere else he's been permitted. He's eaten his first meal at home and relieved himself in the proper place. He's heard lots of new sounds, smelled new friends and seen more of the outside world than ever before...and that was just the first day! He's worn out and is ready for bed...or so you think!

It's puppy's first night home and you are ready to say "Good night." Keep in mind that this is his first night ever to be sleeping alone. His dam and littermates are no longer at paw's length and he's a bit scared, cold and lonely. Be reassuring to your new family member, but this is not the time to spoil him and give in to his inevitable whining.

Puppies whine. They whine to let others know where they are and hopefully to get company out of it. Place your pup in his new bed or crate in his designated area and close the crate door. Mercifully, he may fall asleep without a peep. When the inevitable occurs, however, ignore the whining—he is fine. Be strong and keep his interest in mind. Do

SKULL & CROSSBONES
Thoroughly puppy-proof your house before bringing your puppy home. Never use cockroach or rodent poisons or plant fertilizers in any area accessible to the puppy. Avoid the use of toilet cleaners. Most dogs are born with "toilet-bowl sonar" and will take a drink if the lid is left open. Also keep the trash secured and out of reach.

not allow yourself to feel guilty and visit the pup. He will fall asleep eventually.

Many breeders recommend placing a piece of bedding from the pup's former home in his new bed so that he recognizes and is comforted by the scent of his littermates. Others still advise placing a hot-water bottle in the bed for warmth. The latter may be a good idea provided the pup doesn't attempt to suckle—he'll get good and wet, and may not fall asleep so fast.

Puppy's first night can be somewhat stressful for both the pup and his new family. Remember that you are setting the tone of nighttime at your house. Unless you want to play with your pup every night at 10 p.m., midnight and 2 a.m., don't initiate

the habit. Your family will thank you, and eventually so will your pup!

PREVENTING PUPPY PROBLEMS

SOCIALIZATION

Now that you have done all of the preparatory work and have helped your pup get accustomed to his new home and family, it is about time for you to have some fun! Socializing your Toy Fox Terrier pup gives you the opportunity to show off your new friend, and your pup gets to reap the benefits of being an adorable creature that people will want to pet and, in general, think is absolutely precious!

Besides getting to know his new family, your puppy should be exposed to other people, animals and situations. This will help him become well adjusted as he grows up and less prone to being timid or fearful of the new things he will encounter. Of course, he must not come into close contact with dogs you don't know well until his course of injections is fully complete.

Your pup's socialization began with the breeder, but now it is your responsibility to continue it. Early socialization is critical, as this is the time when he forms his impressions of the outside world. The eight-to-ten-week-old period is also known as the fear period;

MANNERS MATTER

During the socialization process, a puppy should meet people, experience different environments and definitely be exposed to other canines. Through playing and interacting with other dogs, your puppy will learn lessons, ranging from controlling the pressure of his jaws by biting his dam and litter-mates to the inner-workings of the canine pack that he will apply to his human relationships for the rest of his life. That is why removing a puppy from the litter too early (before eight weeks) can be detrimental to the pup's development.

of course includes human contact, affection, handling and exposure to other animals. Once your pup has received his necessary vaccinations, feel free to take him out and about (on his leash, of course). Walk him around the neighborhood, take him on your daily errands, let people pet him, let him meet other dogs and pets, etc. Puppies do not have to try to make friends; there will be no shortage of people who will want to introduce themselves. Just make sure that you carefully supervise each meeting.

If the neighborhood children want to say hello, for example, that is great—children and pups most often make great companions. However, sometimes an excited child can unintentionally handle a pup too roughly, or an overzealous pup can playfully nip a little too hard. You want to make socialization experiences positive ones. What a pup learns during this very formative stage will affect his attitude toward future encounters. You want your dog to be comfortable around everyone. A pup that has a bad experience with a child may grow up to be a dog that is shy around or aggressive toward children.

CONSISTENCY IN TRAINING

Dogs, being pack animals, naturally need a leader, or else they try to establish dominance in their packs. When you welcome a dog

during this time, the interaction he receives should be especially gentle and reassuring.

Lack of socialization, and/or negative experiences during the socialization period, can manifest itself in fear and aggression as the dog grows up. Your puppy needs lots of positive interaction, which into your family, the choice of who becomes the leader and who becomes the "pack" is entirely up to you! Your pup's intuitive quest for dominance, coupled with the fact that it is nearly impossible to look at an adorable Toy Fox Terrier pup with his "puppy-dog" eyes and not cave in, give the pup almost an unfair advantage in getting the upper hand!

A pup will definitely test the waters to see what he can and cannot do. Do not give in to those pleading eyes—stand your ground when it comes to disciplining the pup and make sure that all family members do the same. It will only confuse the pup if Mother tells him to get off the sofa when he is used to sitting up there with Father to watch the nightly news. Avoid discrepancies by having all members of the household decide on the rules before the pup even comes home…and be consistent in enforcing them! Early training shapes the dog's personality, so you cannot be unclear in what you expect.

COMMON PUPPY PROBLEMS

The best way to prevent puppy problems is to be proactive in stopping an undesirable behavior as soon as it starts. The old saying "You can't teach an old dog new tricks" does not necessarily hold true, but it *is* true that it is much easier to discourage bad behavior

Toy Fox Terriers are rarely dog-aggressive and, with proper socialization, can be raised with other dogs. This duo has been close friends for many years.

in a young developing pup than to wait until the pup's bad behavior becomes the adult dog's bad habit. There are some problems that are especially prevalent in puppies as they develop.

NIPPING

As puppies start to teethe, they feel the need to sink their teeth into anything available…unfortunately, that usually includes your fingers, arms, hair and toes. You may find this behavior cute for the first five seconds…until you feel just how sharp those puppy teeth are. Nipping is something you want to discourage immediately and consistently with a firm "No!" (or whatever number of firm "Nos" it takes for him to understand that you mean business). Then, replace your finger with an appropriate chew toy. While this behavior is merely annoying when the dog is young, it can become dangerous as your Toy Fox Terrier's adult teeth grow in and his jaws develop, and he continues to think it is okay to gnaw on human appendages. Your Toy Fox Terrier does not mean any harm with a friendly nip, but he also does not know his own strength.

CHEWING TIPS

Chewing goes hand in hand with nipping in the sense that a teething puppy is always looking for a way to soothe his aching gums. In this case, instead of chewing on you, he may have taken a liking to your favorite shoe or something else that he should not be chewing. Again, realize that this is a normal canine behavior that does not need to be discouraged, only redirected. Your pup just needs to be taught what is acceptable to

chew on and what is off-limits. Consistently tell him "No!" when you catch him chewing on something forbidden and give him a chew toy.

Conversely, praise him when you catch him chewing on something appropriate. In this way, you are discouraging the inappropriate behavior and reinforcing the desired behavior. The puppy's chewing should stop after his adult teeth have come in, but an adult dog continues to chew for various reasons—perhaps because he is bored, needs to relieve tension or just likes to chew. That is why it is important to redirect his chewing when he is still young.

CRYING/WHINING

Your pup will often cry, whine, whimper, howl or make some type of commotion when he is left alone. This is basically his way of calling out for attention to make sure that you know he is there and that you have not forgotten about him. Your puppy feels insecure when he is left alone, when you are out of the house and he is in his crate or when you are in another part of the house and he cannot see you. The noise he is making is an expression of the anxiety he feels at being alone, so he needs to be taught that being alone is okay. You are not actually training the dog to stop making noise; rather, you are training him to feel comfortable when he is alone and thus removing the need for him to make the noise.

This is where the crate with cozy bedding and a toy comes in handy. You want to know that your pup is safe when you are not there to supervise, and you know that he will be safe in his crate rather than roaming freely about the house. In order for the pup to stay in his crate without making a fuss, he first needs to be comfortable in his crate. On that note, it is extremely important that the crate is never used as a form of punishment; this will cause the pup to view the crate as a negative place, rather than as a place of his own for safety and retreat.

Accustom the pup to the crate

Don't leave your Toy Fox waiting by the door! Take him with you whenever you can and spend quality time with him at home.

in short, gradually increasing time intervals in which you put him in the crate, maybe with a treat, and stay in the room with him. If he cries or makes a fuss, do not go to him, but stay in his sight. Gradually he will realize that staying in his crate is just fine without your help, and it will not be so traumatic for him when you are not around. You may want to leave the radio on softly when you leave the house; the sound of human voices may be comforting to him.

FEEDING CONSIDERATIONS

Every breeder of every breed has his own particular way of feeding. Most breeders give the new owner a written record (diet sheet) that details the amount and kind of food that the puppy has been receiving. The diet sheet should also indicate the number of times per day that your puppy has been accustomed to being fed and the kind of vitamin supplementation, if any, he has been receiving. Follow these recommendations to the letter, at least for the first month or two after the puppy comes to live with you. Following the prescribed procedure will reduce the chance of upset stomach and loose stools.

Usually a breeder's diet sheet projects the increases and changes in food that will be necessary as your puppy grows from week to week. If the sheet does not include this information, ask the breeder for suggestions regarding increases and eventual changes.

If you do your best not to change the puppy's diet when you first bring him home, you will be less apt to run into digestive problems and diarrhea. Diarrhea is very serious in young puppies. Puppies with diarrhea can dehydrate very rapidly, causing severe problems and even death.

STORING DOG FOOD

You must store your dry dog food carefully. Open packages of dog food quickly lose their vitamin value, usually within 90 days of being opened. Mold spores and vermin could also contaminate the food.

If it is necessary to change your Toy Fox Terrier puppy's diet for any reason, it should be done gradually, over a period of several meals and a few days. Begin by adding a spoonful or two of the new food, gradually increasing the amount until the meal consists entirely of the new product.

Most commercial foods manufactured for dogs meet government standards and prove this by listing the ingredients contained in the food on every package or can. The ingredients are listed in descending order, with the main ingredient listed first.

Fed with any regularity at all, refined sugars can cause your Toy Fox Terrier to become obese and will definitely create tooth decay. Candy stores do not exist in the wild and canine teeth are not genetically disposed to handling sugars. Do not feed your Toy Fox Terrier candy or sweets and avoid products that contain sugar to any high degree. Aside from being high in sugar, chocolate is particularly dangerous as it contains a chemical that is toxic to dogs and can cause death even in small amounts.

Fresh water and a properly prepared, balanced diet containing the essential nutrients in correct proportions are all a healthy Toy Fox Terrier needs to be offered. Dog foods come in

TEST FOR PROPER DIET
A good test for proper diet is the color, odor and firmness of your dog's stool. A healthy dog usually produces three semi-hard stools per day. The stools should have no unpleasant odor. They should be the same color from excretion to excretion.

many varieties, including canned, dry, semi-moist, "scientifically fortified" and "all-natural." A visit to your local supermarket or pet store will reveal from how vast an array you will be able to select.

It is important to remember that all dogs, whether Toy Fox Terriers or Great Danes, are carnivorous (meat-eating) animals. While the vegetable content of your Toy Fox Terrier's diet should not be overlooked, a

FOOD PREFERENCE

Selecting the best dry dog food is difficult. There is no majority consensus among veterinary scientists as to the value of nutrient analysis (protein, fat, fiber, moisture, ash, cholesterol, minerals, etc.). All agree that feeding trials are what matter most, but you also have to consider the individual dog. The dog's weight, age and activity level, and what pleases his taste, all must be considered. It is probably best to take the advice of your veterinarian. Every dog's dietary requirements vary, even during the lifetime of a particular dog.

If your dog is fed a good dry food, he does not require supplements of meat or vegetables. Dogs do appreciate a little variety in their diets, so you may choose to stay with the same brand but vary the flavor. Alternatively, you may wish to add a little flavored stock to give a difference to the taste.

dog's physiology and anatomy are based upon carnivorous food acquisition. Protein and fat are absolutely essential to the well-being of your dog. In fact, it is wise to add a teaspoon or two of vegetable oil or bacon drippings to your dog's diet, particularly during the winter months in colder climates.

Through centuries of domestication, we have made our dogs entirely dependent upon us for their well-being. Therefore, we are entirely responsible for duplicating the food balance that the wild dog finds in Nature. The domesticated dog's diet must include protein, carbohydrates, fats, roughage and small amounts of essential minerals and vitamins.

Finding commercially prepared diets that contain all of the necessary nutrients will not present a problem. It is important to understand, though, that these commercially prepared foods contain the *complete* nutrition that your Toy Fox Terrier needs. It is therefore unnecessary to add vitamin supplements to these diets except in special circumstances as prescribed by your veterinarian. Over-supplementation and forced growth are now looked upon by some breeders as major contributors to many skeletal abnormalities found in pure-bred dogs of the day.

A great deal of controversy

exists today regarding orthopedic problems such as hip dysplasia and patellar (knee) luxation, which are found in many breeds and can afflict all breeds. Some claim that these problems are entirely hereditary conditions, but many others feel that they can be exacerbated by over-use of mineral and vitamin supplements for puppies.

In giving vitamin supplementation, you should never exceed the prescribed amount. Many Toy Fox Terrier breeders insist that all recommended dosages be halved before including them in a dog's diet. Still other breeders feel that no supplementation should be given at all, believing a balanced diet that includes animal protein, plenty of milk products, some fat and a small amount of bone meal to provide calcium are all that are necessary and beneficial.

Pregnant and lactating bitches may require supplementation of some kind, but here again it is not a case of "if a little is good, a lot would be a great deal better." Extreme caution is advised in this case and of course you should consult with your veterinarian before giving any supplements.

There are now a number of commercially prepared diets for dogs with special dietary needs. Overweight, underweight and geriatric dogs can have their

FEEDING TIPS

- Dog food must be served at room temperature, neither too hot nor too cold. Fresh water, changed often and served in a clean bowl, is mandatory, especially when feeding dry food.
- Never feed your dog from the table while you are eating, and never feed your dog leftovers from your own meal. They usually contain too much fat and too much seasoning.
- Dogs must chew their food. Hard pellets are excellent; soups and stews are to be avoided.
- Don't add leftovers or any extras to complete commercial dog food. This type of food should be balanced, and adding something extra destroys the balance.
- Except for age-related changes, dogs do not require dietary variations. They can be fed the same diet, day after day, without becoming bored or ill.

nutritional needs met, as can puppies and growing dogs. The calorie content of these foods is adjusted accordingly. With the correct amount of the right foods and the proper amount of exercise, your Toy Fox Terrier should stay in top shape. Again, common sense must prevail. Just as in humans, too many calories will increase weight and cutting back on calories will reduce weight.

By and large, Toy Fox Terriers are good eaters but occasionally a young Toy Fox Terrier going through the teething period or a female coming into season will lose interest in food. The concerned owner's first response is often to tempt the dog by hand-feeding special treats and foods that the problem eater seems to prefer. This practice only serves to compound the problem. Once a dog learns to play the waiting game, he will turn up his nose at anything other than his favorite food, knowing full well that what he wants to eat will eventually arrive.

When selecting your dog's diet, three stages of development must be considered: the puppy stage, the adult stage and the senior stage.

PUPPY STAGE
Puppies instinctively want to suck milk from their mother's teats; a normal puppy will exhibit this behavior just a few moments following birth. If puppies do not attempt to suckle within the first half-hour or so, the breeder should encourage them to do so by placing them on the nipples, having selected ones with plenty of milk. This early milk supply is important in providing the essential colostrum, which protects the puppies during the first eight to ten weeks of their lives. Although a mother's milk is much better than any commercially prepared milk formula, despite there being some excellent ones available, if the puppies do not feed, the breeder will have to feed them by hand. For those with less experience, advice from a veterinarian is important so that not only the right quantity of milk is fed but also that of correct quality, fed at suitably frequent intervals, usually every two hours during the first few days of life.

Puppies should be allowed to nurse from their mothers for about the first six weeks, although, starting around the third or fourth week, the breeder will begin to introduce small portions of suitable solid food. Most breeders like to introduce alternate milk and meat meals initially, building up to weaning time.

By the time the puppies are seven or a maximum of eight

Since you should monitor how much food your Toy Fox Terrier puppy is eating, free-feeding is not recommended. Adult dogs, however, can be allowed to free-feed once they have reached their mature size.

weeks old, they should be fully weaned and fed solely on a proprietary puppy food. Selection of the most suitable, good-quality diet at this time is essential, for a puppy's fastest growth rate is during the first year of life. The frequency of meals will be reduced over time, and most breeders recommend the transition from growth-formula food to adult-maintenance diet after the puppy has reached six months of age, although most wait until nine months of age. Puppy and junior diets should be well balanced for the needs of your dog so that, except in certain circumstances, additional vitamins, minerals and proteins will not be required.

ADULT DIETS
A dog is considered an adult when he has stopped growing. In the Toy Fox, full maturity and size vary widely from bloodline to bloodline. Many will have completed their full growth by nine months of age, while others continue to grow until they are a year old. Increases in size even as

late as 18–20 months of age have been reported. Therefore, there is no hard and fast rule as to when a Toy Fox reaches adulthood. As previously stated, breeders generally advise switching puppies to an adult diet after six months of age, with most waiting until nine months of age. Of course, any questions you have about when to change the diet or the suitability of the new food can be answered by your breeder or vet.

Major dog-food manufacturers specialize in adult-maintenance food, so it is merely necessary for you to select the one best suited to your dog's needs. For example, active dogs will have different requirements than sedate dogs. Depending upon the individual dog and his general condition (weight, activity, etc.), the maintenance diet can be used with most Toy Fox Terriers until seven years of age or even older.

Senior Diets

As dogs get older, their metabolism changes. The older dog usually exercises less, moves more slowly and sleeps more. This change in lifestyle and physiological performance requires a change in diet. Since these changes take place slowly, they might not be recognizable. What is easily recognizable is weight gain. By continuing to feed your dog an adult-maintenance diet when he is slowing down metabolically, your dog will gain weight. Obesity in an older dog compounds the health problems that already accompany old age.

As your dog gets older, few of his organs function up to par. The kidneys slow down and the intestines become less efficient. These age-related factors are best handled with a change in diet and a change in feeding schedule to give smaller portions that are more easily digested. Eight years old is usually the average age at which to consider a dog to have reached "senior status."

There is no single best diet for every older dog. While many dogs do well on light or senior diets, other dogs do better on puppy diets or other special premium diets such as lamb and rice. Be sensitive to your senior Toy Fox Terrier's diet, as this will help control other problems that may arise with your old friend.

WATER

Just as your dog needs proper nutrition from his food, water is an essential "nutrient" as well. Water keeps the dog's body properly hydrated and promotes normal function of the body's systems. During the housebreaking process, it is necessary to keep an eye on how much water your Toy Fox Terrier is drinking, but once he is reliably trained he should have access to clean fresh

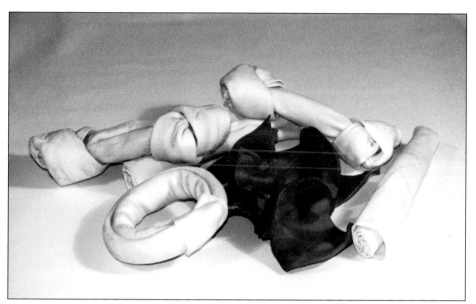

Organic dog chews, like rawhide and pig ears, usually delight Toy Fox Terriers, as most of them are active chewers. Chews that are packaged are more sanitary than loose items.

water at all times, especially if you feed dry food only. Make certain that the dog's water bowl is clean, and change the water often.

EXERCISE
Most Toy Fox Terriers are self-exercisers and will get all the exercise they need in the home and yard—walking, standing guard, investigating and following their loved ones around. This is not to say that they won't enjoy and benefit from morning walks, games of retrieving balls in the fenced yard, hikes over mountain trails or exploring tide pools along the beach. On the other hand, if your own exercise proclivities lie closer to a nice walk around the block than to a long run, your Toy Fox will be just as satisfied. The Toy Fox Terrier is not a breed that requires taking your energy level to its outer limits.

Most Toy Fox Terriers are very "busy" dogs and, if your Toy Fox shares his life with young children or other dogs, he could easily be getting all the exercise he needs to stay fit. The Toy Fox Terrier is always ready for a romp with a playmate or to invent some new game that entails plenty of aerobic activity.

Slow steady exercise that keeps your companion's heart rate in the working range will do nothing but extend the dog's life. If your Toy Fox Terrier is getting his needed activity with you at his side, you are increasing the

DRINK, DRANK, DRUNK— MAKE IT A DOUBLE

In both humans and dogs, as well as other living organisms, water forms the major part of nearly every body tissue. Naturally, we take water for granted, but without it, life as we know it would cease.

For dogs, water is needed to keep their bodies functioning biochemically. Additionally, water is needed to replace the water lost while panting. Unlike humans, who are able to sweat to dissipate heat, dogs must pant to cool down, thereby losing the vital water from their bodies need to regulate their body temperatures. Humans lose electrolyte-containing products and other body-fluid components through sweating; dogs do not lose anything except water.

Water is essential always, but especially so when the weather is hot or humid or when your dog is exercising or working vigorously.

chances that the two of you will enjoy each other's company for many more years to come.

Naturally, common sense must prevail regarding the extent and the intensity of the exercise you give your Toy Fox Terrier. Remember that young puppies have short bursts of energy and then require long rest periods. Again—short exercise periods and long rest stops for any Toy Fox Terrier under 12 months of age. Young dogs and puppies must be kept from jumping on and off chairs, climbing steps, etc. Young bones are extremely fragile, and this should be kept in mind with all exercise that you do with your Toy Fox under one year of age.

Most adult Toy Fox Terriers will willingly walk as far as, perhaps further than, their owners are inclined to go; this even applies to elderly dogs. Daily walks, combined with moderated game-playing in the yard, can keep even the most senior Toy Fox Terrier in fine fettle. Remember, if playing games or walking with the Toy Fox at any age, that he must be kept on-leash or in a securely fenced area. You want your dog to run, not to run away!

Caution and common sense must be exercised in hot weather, of course, with dogs of all ages, young and old. Plan your walks for the first thing in the morning if at all possible. If you can not arrange to do this, wait until the sun has set and the outdoor temperature has dropped to a comfortable degree.

Cold weather is no problem for the Toy Fox Terrier, who has his own little jacket, if he is kept active. However, do not push your Toy Fox Terrier out the door in freezing weather and forget that he's there! The breed does not have the protective undercoat to protect him in that kind of weather.

Do not allow your Toy Fox Terrier to remain wet if the two of you get caught in the rain while out walking. At the very least, you should towel-dry the wet Toy Fox Terrier. Better still, use your blow dryer, on the lowest setting, to make sure that your Toy Fox Terrier is thoroughly dry on those damp and chilly days.

Bear in mind that an overweight dog should never be suddenly over-exercised; instead, he should be encouraged to increase exercise slowly. Also remember that not only is exercise essential to keep the dog's body fit, it is essential to his mental well-being. A bored dog will find something to do, which often manifests itself in some type of destructive behavior. In this sense, exercise is essential for the owner's mental well-being as well!

EXERCISE ALERT!
You should be careful where you exercise your dog. Many areas have been sprayed with chemicals that are highly toxic to both dogs and humans. Never allow your dog to eat grass or drink from puddles on either public or private grounds, as the run-off water may contain chemicals from sprays and herbicides.

GROOMING

Regular brushing using a soft-bristled brush and bathing on the rare occasions that the need arises are all the grooming that your Toy Fox Terrier's coat will ever need. Even if yours is a show dog, the Toy Fox Terrier is shown *au naturel*—although your breeder will undoubtedly be happy to show you a few "tricks of the trade" that will help make your little fellow look picture-pretty.

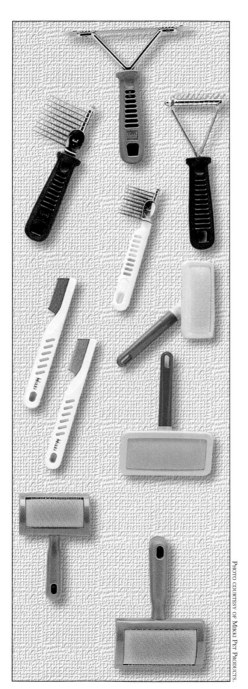

Toy Fox Terriers require little grooming, but they should be brushed to remove dead hair and dirt and to stimulate the dog's natural oils.

Brushing is effective for removing dirt and dead hair, and stimulating the dog's natural oils to add shine and a healthy look to the coat. Although the Toy Fox Terrier's coat is short and close, it does require a five-minute once-over on a regular basis to keep it looking its shiny best. Grooming sessions are also a good way to spend time with your dog. Many dogs grow to like the feel of being brushed and will enjoy the routine.

BATHING

It is neither necessary nor recommended to bathe your Toy Fox Terrier frequently, but it is inevitable that the need for a bath will arise once in a while. Again, like most anything, if you introduce your pup to the bath as a puppy, it will be easier for both of you when he is an adult. You want your dog to be at ease in the bath or else it could end up a wet, soapy, messy ordeal for both of you!

Brush your Toy Fox Terrier thoroughly before wetting his coat. This will get rid of any debris and dead hair, which are easier to remove when the coat is dry. Put your Toy Fox in the basin, making certain that he has a good non-slip surface on which to stand. Begin by wetting the dog's coat, checking the water temperature to make sure that it is neither too hot nor too cold for the dog. A shower or hose attachment is necessary for thoroughly wetting and rinsing the coat.

Next, apply shampoo to the dog's coat and work it into a good lather. Wash the head last, as you do not want shampoo to drip into the dog's eyes while you are washing the rest of his body. You should use only a shampoo that is made for dogs. Do not use a product made for human hair. Work the shampoo all the way down to the skin. You can use this opportunity to check the skin for any bumps, bites or other abnormalities. Do not neglect any area of the body—get all of the hard-to-reach places.

Once the dog has been thoroughly shampooed, he requires an equally thorough rinsing. Shampoo left in the coat can be irritating to the dog's skin. Protect his eyes from the shampoo by shielding them with your hand and directing the flow of water in the opposite direction. You also should avoid getting water in the ear canal. Be prepared for your dog to shake out his coat—you might want to stand back, but make sure you have a hold on the dog to keep him from running through the house.

Have an absorbent towel on hand to soak up most of the water from your dog's coat. You may want to finish the job with a blow dryer. Use only the lowest

PRICK UP YOUR EARS
Most Toy Fox Terriers have upright ears that are broad and open to the air. For health and maintenance purposes, pricked ears are preferred. In addition to being more open to the air, they are also easier to keep clean. Dogs with natural drop ears often succumb to bacterial problems, largely due to a damp, dark outer ear that is not kept clean and dry. Probing in the dog's ear with a cotton swab is not recommended as it can be dangerous if not done with extreme care.

heat setting, as you do not want to burn the dog's skin while drying. It is important to dry the dog thoroughly, especially in colder weather.

EAR CLEANING

The ears should be kept clean with a cotton ball and ear powder or liquid made especially for dogs. Do not probe into the ear canal with anything, as this can cause injury. Be on the lookout for any signs of infection or ear-

BATHING BEAUTY

Once you are sure that the dog is thoroughly rinsed, squeeze the excess water out of his coat with your hand and dry him with a heavy towel. You may choose to use a blow dryer on low heat on his coat or just let it dry naturally. In cold weather, never allow your dog outside with a wet coat.

There are "dry bath" products on the market, which are sprays and powders intended for spot cleaning, that can be used between regular baths if necessary. They are not substitutes for regular baths, but they are easy to use for touch-ups as they do not require rinsing.

mite infestation. If your Toy Fox Terrier has been shaking his head or scratching at his ears frequently, this usually indicates a problem. If the dog's ears have an unusual odor, this is a sure sign of mite infestation or infection, and a signal to have his ears checked by the veterinarian.

NAIL CLIPPING

Grooming time is the best time to accustom your Toy Fox Terrier to having his nails trimmed and his feet inspected. Always inspect your dog's feet for cracked pads. Check between the toes for splinters and thorns. Pay particular attention to any swollen or tender areas.

The nails of a Toy Fox Terrier who spends most of his time indoors or on grass when outdoors can grow long very quickly. Do not allow your dog's nails to become overgrown and then expect to cut them back easily.

Each nail has a blood vessel running through the center called the "quick." The quick grows close to the end of the nail and contains very sensitive nerve endings. If the nail is allowed to grow too long, it will be impossible to cut it back to a proper length without cutting into the quick. This causes severe pain to the dog and can also result in a great deal of bleeding that can be very difficult to stop.

If your Toy Fox Terrier is getting plenty of exercise on cement or rough hard pavement, the nails may be sufficiently worn down on their own. Otherwise, the nails must be trimmed with nail clippers made expressly for dogs. These clippers can be purchased at pet-supply stores.

Hold your dog's foot in your hand and proceed with caution, removing only a small portion of the nail at a time. Should the quick be nipped in the trimming process, there are any number of blood-clotting products available at pet shops (or you can use those that a person uses for shaving) that will almost immediately stem the flow of blood. It is wise to have one of these products on hand in case there is a nail-trimming accident or the dog tears a nail on his own.

You will find that most Toy Fox Terriers will not have nail clipping on their lists of favorite things to do! In fact, you may find that having someone to help you makes the job much easier on both you and the dog—one person to hold the dog, the other to clip. Also, the earlier in life that you accustom your Toy Fox to nail clipping, the less of a problem it will be as the dog grows up. Nail maintenance will be part of your grooming routine throughout the dog's life. A dog's long nails can scratch someone

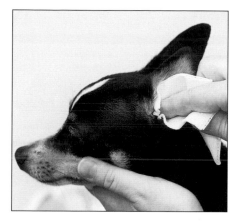

The ears should be cleaned weekly with ear powder or liquid and a soft cotton wipe.

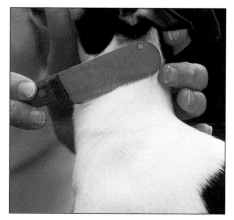

A flea comb is ideal for removing any parasites from your Toy Fox Terrier's coat. This type of metal comb has short teeth that penetrate through the coat to reach the skin.

A soft-bristle brush or a hound glove is ideal for giving the Toy Fox's short coat a weekly once-over.

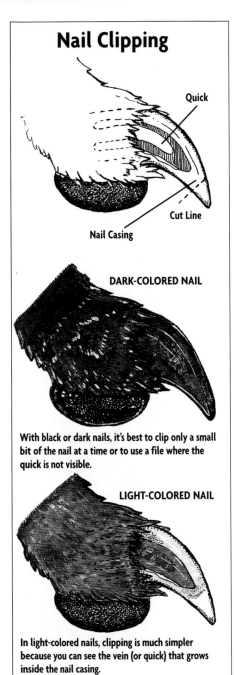

Nail Clipping

Quick

Cut Line

Nail Casing

DARK-COLORED NAIL

With black or dark nails, it's best to clip only a small bit of the nail at a time or to use a file where the quick is not visible.

LIGHT-COLORED NAIL

In light-colored nails, clipping is much simpler because you can see the vein (or quick) that grows inside the nail casing.

unintentionally and also have a better chance of ripping and bleeding, or causing the feet to spread. A good rule of thumb is that if you can hear your dog's nails' clicking on the floor when he walks, his nails are too long.

DENTAL CARE

Most toy breeds have dental problems and will often suffer from early tooth loss. Toy Fox Terriers are no exception. You can help stave off these problems by providing your dog with hard dog biscuits and chews in the sizes meant just for the toy breeds. Chewing helps keep tartar and plaque from forming. Build-up of either of these can cause extensive and permanent damage to the teeth and gums.

Brushing your dog's teeth at least two or three time a week can prevent tooth decay and the necessity of having your veterinarian take care of advanced problems under anesthesia. You will brush your dog's teeth in the same manner as you brush your own, but using tooth-brushing products made especially for dogs. The pastes and powders we use on our own teeth most often contain sugars that will do more harm than good.

Will your Toy Fox Terrier allow you to brush his teeth? But of course! Your dog is well trained and you started doing this with him in puppyhood.

TRAVELING WITH YOUR DOG

CAR TRAVEL

You should accustom your Toy Fox Terrier to riding in a car at an early age. You may or may not take him in the car often, but at the very least he will need to go to the vet and you do not want these trips to be traumatic for the dog or troublesome for you. The safest way for a dog to ride in the car is in his crate. If he uses a crate in the house, you can use the same crate for travel or a separate travel crate.

Put the pup in the crate and see how he reacts. If he seems uneasy, you can have a passenger hold him on his lap while you drive. Regardless, do not let the dog roam loose in the vehicle—this is very dangerous! If you should stop short, your dog can be thrown and injured. If the dog starts climbing on you and pestering you while you are driving, you will not be able to concentrate on the road. It is an unsafe situation for everyone—human and canine.

For long trips, be prepared to stop to let the dog relieve himself. Take with you whatever you need to clean up after him, including some paper towels and perhaps some old bath towels or rags for use should he have a

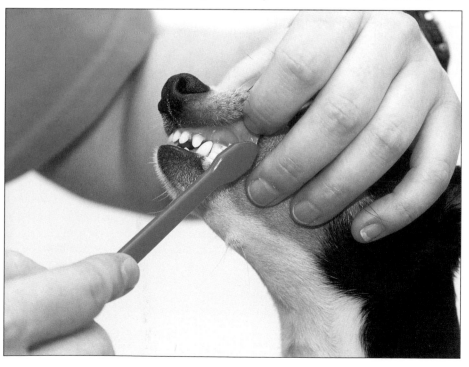

Brushing your dog's teeth is quite simple, but must be started when the dog is still a puppy. Use instruments and products made specifically for dogs.

Use your dog's crate whenever traveling in the car. This is the safest and least troublesome method of car travel with your Toy Fox Terrier.

potty accident in the car or suffer from motion sickness.

Remember that *no dog should ever be left in a car in hot weather!* Temperatures can soar in a matter of minutes and your dog can die of heat exhaustion in less time than you would ever imagine. Rolling down the windows helps little and is dangerous at any time, but an overheated dog will surely panic and attempt to escape through the open window. A word to the wise—leave your dog at home in a cool room on hot days.

Air Travel

Check in advance with your chosen airline before proceeding with air travel plans that include your Toy Fox Terrier, as arrangements will have to be made ahead of time and you'll need to comply with all of the airline's regulations. For example, the dog will be required to travel in a fiberglass crate that meets specific requirements of size, type and labeling, and you will also need to provide current health documentation.

As the owner of a Toy Fox Terrier, you are lucky in that you probably will be able to "carry on" your dog in his crate, as many airlines allow small breeds to travel with their owners in the cabin of the plane. To help put the dog at ease, give your dog one of his favorite toys in the crate. Do not feed the dog for several hours before the trip in order to minimize his need to relieve himself. However, certain airlines require you to provide documentation as to when the dog has last been fed. In any case, a light meal is best.

Make sure that your dog is properly identified and that your contact information appears on his ID tags and on his crate. Although your Toy Fox should be permitted to travel in the same part of the plane that you do, every rule still must be strictly followed to prevent the risk of getting separated from your dog.

VACATIONS AND BOARDING

So you want to take a family vacation—and you want to include *all* members of the family. You would probably make arrangements for accommodations ahead of time anyway, but this is especially important when traveling with a dog. You do not want to make an overnight stop at the only place around for miles, only to find out that they do not allow dogs. Also, you do not want to reserve a place for your family without confirming that you are traveling with a dog, because, if it is against the hotel's policy, you may end up without a place to stay.

Alternatively, if you are traveling and choose not to bring your Toy Fox Terrier, you will have to make arrangements for

COLLAR REQUIRED

If your dog gets lost, he is not able to ask for directions home. Identification tags fastened to the collar give important information—the dog's name, the owner's name, the owner's address and a telephone number where the owner can be reached. This makes it easy for whomever finds the dog to contact the owner and arrange to have the dog returned. An added advantage is that a person will be more likely to approach a lost dog who has ID tags on his collar; it tells the person that this is somebody's pet rather than a stray. This is the easiest and fastest method of identification, provided that the tags stay on the collar and the collar stays on the dog.

Visit local boarding kennels before you actually need to use one's services. Look for cleanliness, roominess and a knowledgeable, caring staff.

him while you are away. Some options are to take him to a friend's house to stay while you are gone, to have a trusted friend stop by often or stay at your house or to bring your dog to a reputable boarding kennel. If you choose to board him at a kennel, you should visit in advance to see the facilities provided and where the dogs are kept. Are the dogs' areas spacious and kept clean? Talk to some of the employees and observe how they treat the dogs—do they spend time with the dogs, play with them, exercise them, etc.? Also find out the kennel's policy on vaccinations and what they require. This is for all of the dogs' safety, since there is a greater risk of diseases being passed from dog to dog when dogs are kept together.

IDENTIFICATION

Your Toy Fox Terrier is your valued companion and friend. That is why you always keep a close eye on him and you have made sure that he cannot escape from the yard or wriggle out of his collar. However, accidents can happen and there may come a time when your dog unexpectedly becomes separated from you. If this unfortunate event should occur, the first thing on your mind will be finding him. Proper identification, including an ID tag, and possibly a tattoo and/or a microchip, will increase the chances of his being returned to you safely and quickly.

IDENTIFICATION OPTIONS

As puppies become more and more expensive, especially those puppies of high quality for showing and/or breeding, they have a greater chance of being stolen. The usual collar dog tag is, of course, easily removed. But there are two more permanent techniques that have become widely used for identifying dogs.

The puppy microchip implantation involves the injection of a small microchip, about the size of a corn kernel, under the skin of the dog. If your dog shows up at a clinic or shelter, or is offered for resale under less-than-savory circumstances, it can be positively identified by the microchip. The microchip is scanned, and a registry quickly identifies you as the owner.

Tattooing is done on various parts of the dog, from his belly to his ears. The number tattooed can be your telephone number, the dog's registration number or any other number that you can easily memorize. When professional dog thieves see a tattooed dog, they usually lose interest. For the safety of our dogs, no laboratory facility or dog broker will accept a tattooed dog as stock.

Discuss microchipping and tattooing with your vet and breeder. Some vets perform these services on their own premises for a reasonable fee. To ensure that the dog's ID is effective, be certain that the dog is then properly registered with a legitimate national database.

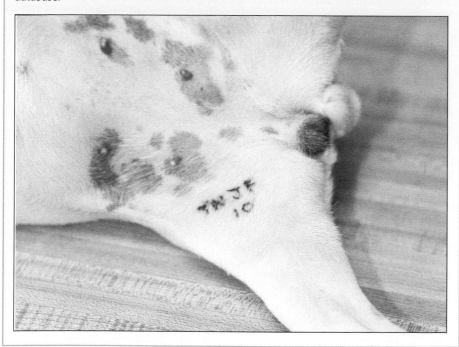

Living with an untrained dog is a lot like owning a piano that you do not know how to play—it is a nice object to look at, but it does not do much more than that to bring you pleasure. Now try taking piano lessons, and suddenly the piano comes alive and brings forth magical sounds and rhythms that set your heart singing and your body swaying.

The same is true with your Toy Fox Terrier. Any dog is a big responsibility and, if not trained sensibly, may develop unacceptable behavior that annoys you or could even cause family friction.

To train your Toy Fox Terrier, you may like to enroll in an obedience class. Teach your dog good manners as you learn how and why he behaves the way he does. Find out how to communicate with your dog and how to recognize and understand his communications with you. Suddenly the dog takes on a new role in your life—he is clever, interesting, well behaved and fun to be with. He demonstrates his bond of devotion to you daily. In other words, your Toy Fox Terrier does wonders for your ego

REAP THE REWARDS
If you start with a normal, healthy dog and give him time, patience and some carefully executed lessons, you will reap the rewards of that training for the life of the dog. And what a life it will be! The two of you will find immeasurable pleasure in the companionship you have built together with love, respect and understanding.

because he constantly reminds you that you are not only his leader, you are his hero!

Those involved with teaching dog obedience and counseling owners about their dogs' behavior have discovered some interesting facts about dog ownership. For example, training dogs when they are puppies results in the highest rate of success in developing well-mannered and well-adjusted adult dogs. Training an older dog, from six months to six years of age, can produce almost equal results, providing that the owner accepts the dog's slower rate of learning capability and is willing to work patiently to help the dog succeed at developing to his fullest potential. Unfortunately, many owners of untrained adult dogs lack the patience factor, so they do not persist until their dogs are successful at learning particular behaviors.

Training a puppy aged 10 to 16 weeks (20 weeks at the most) is like working with a dry sponge in a pool of water. The pup soaks up whatever you show him and constantly looks for more things to do and learn. At this early age, his body is not yet producing hormones, and therein lies the reason for such a high rate of success. Without hormones, he is focused on his owners and not particularly interested in investigating other places, dogs, people, etc. You are his leader: his

PARENTAL GUIDANCE
Training a dog is a life experience. Many parents admit that much of what they know about raising children they learned from caring for their dogs. Dogs respond to love, fairness and guidance, just as children do. Become a good dog owner and you may become an even better parent.

provider of food, water, shelter and security. He latches onto you and wants to stay close. He will usually follow you from room to room, will not let you out of his sight when you are outdoors with him and will respond in like manner to the people and animals you encounter. If you greet a friend warmly, he will be happy to greet the person as well. If, however, you are hesitant or anxious about the approach of a stranger, he will respond accordingly.

Once the puppy begins to produce hormones, his natural curiosity emerges and he begins to investigate the world around him. It is at this time when you may notice that the untrained dog begins to wander away from you and even ignore your commands to stay close. When this behavior becomes a problem, you have two choices: get rid of the dog or train him. It is strongly urged that you choose the latter option.

You usually will be able to find obedience classes within a reasonable distance from your home, but you can also do a lot to train your dog yourself. Sometimes there are classes available, but the tuition is too costly. Whatever the circumstances, the solution to training your dog without formal lessons lies within the pages of this book.

This chapter is devoted to helping you train your Toy Fox Terrier at home. If the recommended procedures are followed faithfully, you may expect positive results that will prove rewarding both to you and your dog. Whether your new charge is a puppy or a mature adult, the methods of teaching and the techniques we use in training basic behaviors are the same. After all,

no dog, whether puppy or adult, likes harsh or inhumane methods. All creatures, however, respond favorably to gentle motivational methods and sincere praise and encouragement.

HOUSEBREAKING
You can train a puppy to relieve himself wherever you choose, but this must be somewhere suitable. You should bear in mind from the outset that when your puppy is old enough to go out in public places, any canine droppings must be removed at once. You will always have to carry with you a small plastic bag or "poop-scoop."

Outdoor training includes such surfaces as grass, soil and cement. Indoor training usually means training your dog to newspaper. When deciding on the surface and location that you will want your Toy Fox Terrier to use, be sure it is going to be permanent. Training your dog to grass and then changing your mind a few months later is extremely difficult for both dog and owner.

Next, choose the command you will use each and every time you want your puppy to void. "Hurry up" and "Let's go" are examples of commands commonly used by dog owners. Get in the habit of giving the puppy your chosen relief command before you take him out. That way, when he becomes

Small breeds like the Toy Fox Terrier can be housebroken on newspapers, though some owners prefer to introduce their dogs to outdoor relief areas right away.

an adult, you will be able to determine if he wants to go out when you ask him. A confirmation will be signs of interest such as wagging his tail, watching you intently, going to the door, etc.

PUPPY'S NEEDS

Your puppy needs to relieve himself after play periods, after each meal, after he has been sleeping and at any time he indicates that he is looking for a place to urinate or defecate. The urinary and intestinal tract muscles of very young puppies are not fully developed. Therefore, like human babies, puppies need to relieve themselves frequently.

Take your puppy out often—every hour for an eight-week-old puppy, for example—and always immediately after sleeping and eating. The older the puppy, the less often he will need to relieve himself. Finally, as a mature healthy adult, he will require only three to five relief trips per day.

CANINE DEVELOPMENT SCHEDULE

It is important to understand how and at what age a puppy develops into adulthood. If you are a puppy owner, consult the following Canine Development Schedule to determine the stage of development your puppy is currently experiencing. This knowledge will help you as you work with the puppy in the weeks and months ahead.

Period	Age	Characteristics
FIRST TO THIRD	BIRTH TO SEVEN WEEKS	Puppy needs food, sleep and warmth, and responds to simple and gentle touching. Needs mother for security and disciplining. Needs littermates for learning and interacting with other dogs. Pup learns to function within a pack and learns pack order of dominance. Begin socializing pup with adults and children for short periods. Pup begins to become aware of his environment.
FOURTH	EIGHT TO TWELVE WEEKS	Brain is fully developed. Needs socializing with outside world. Remove from mother and littermates. Needs to change from canine pack to human pack. Human dominance necessary. Fear period occurs between 8 and 12 weeks. Avoid fright and pain.
FIFTH	THIRTEEN TO SIXTEEN WEEKS	Training and formal obedience should begin. Less association with other dogs, more with people, places, situations. Period will pass easily if you remember that this is pup's change-to-adolescence time. Be firm and fair. Flight instinct prominent. Permissiveness and over-disciplining can do permanent damage. Praise for good behavior.
JUVENILE	FOUR TO EIGHT MONTHS	Another fear period about 7 to 8 months of age. It passes quickly, but be cautious of fright and pain. Sexual maturity reached. Dominant traits established. Dog should understand sit, down, come and stay by now.

NOTE: THESE ARE APPROXIMATE TIME FRAMES. ALLOW FOR INDIVIDUAL DIFFERENCES IN PUPPIES.

HOUSING

Since the types of housing and control you provide for your puppy have a direct relationship on the success of housebreaking, we consider the various aspects of both before we begin training. Taking a new puppy home and turning him loose in your house can be compared to turning a child loose in an amusement park telling the child that the place is all his! The sheer enormity of the place would be too much for him to handle. Instead, offer the puppy clearly defined areas where he can play, sleep, eat and live. A room of the house where the family gathers is the most obvious choice. Puppies are social animals and need to feel a part of the pack right from the start. Hearing your voice, watching you while you are doing things and smelling you nearby are all positive reinforcers that he is now a member of your pack. Usually a family room, the kitchen or a nearby adjoining breakfast area is ideal for providing safety and security for both puppy and owner.

Within the designated room, there should be a smaller area that the puppy can call his own. An alcove, a wire or fiberglass dog crate or a partitioned-off (not boarded!) corner from which he can view the activities of his new family will be fine. The size of the area or crate is the key factor here.

With patience and consistency, even a young person can train a Toy Fox Terrier to become a clean, obedient home companion.

The area must be large enough so that the puppy can lie down and stretch out, as well as stand up, without rubbing his head on the top. At the same time, it must be small enough so that he cannot relieve himself at one end and sleep at the other without coming into contact with his droppings during the housebreaking process, before he is fully trained. Dogs are, by nature, clean animals and will not remain close to their relief areas unless forced to do so. In those cases, they then become dirty dogs and usually remain that way for life.

The dog's designated area should contain clean bedding and a toy. Avoid putting water or food in the dog's crate or area before he is fully housebroken, as drinking and eating will activate his digestive processes and ultimately defeat your purpose, not to mention make the puppy very uncomfortable if he's always trying to "hold it."

CONTROL
By *control*, we mean helping the puppy to create a lifestyle pattern

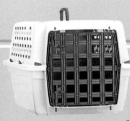

THE SUCCESS METHOD

Success that comes by luck is usually short-lived. Success that comes by well-thought-out proven methods is often more easily achieved and permanent. This is the Success Method. It is designed to give you, the puppy owner, a simple yet proven way to help your puppy develop clean living habits and a feeling of security in his new environment.

6 Steps to Successful Crate Training

1 Tell the puppy "Crate time!" and place him in the crate with a small treat (a piece of cheese or half of a biscuit). Let him stay in the crate for five minutes while you are in the same room. Then release him and praise lavishly. Never release him when he is fussing. Wait until he is quiet before you let him out.

2 Repeat Step 1 several times a day.

3 The next day, place the puppy in the crate as before. Let him stay there for ten minutes. Do this several times.

4 Continue building time in five-minute increments until the puppy stays in his crate for 30 minutes with you in the room. Always take him to his relief area after prolonged periods in his crate.

5 Now go back to Step 1 and let the puppy stay in his crate for five minutes, this time while you are out of the room.

6 Once again, build crate time in five-minute increments with you out of the room. When the puppy will stay willingly in his crate (he may even fall asleep!) for 30 minutes with you out of the room, he will be ready to stay in it for several hours at a time.

that will be compatible to that of his human pack (*you*!). Just as we guide little children to learn our way of life, we must show the puppy when it is time to play, eat, sleep, exercise and even entertain himself.

Your puppy should always sleep In his crate. He should also learn that, during times of household confusion and excessive human activity, such as at breakfast when family members are preparing for the day, he can play by himself in relative safety and comfort in his designated area. Each time you leave the puppy alone, he should understand exactly where he is to stay.

Puppies are chewers and cannot tell the difference between lamp and television wires, shoes, table legs, etc. Chewing into a television wire, for example, can be fatal to the puppy, while a shorted wire can start a fire in the house. If the puppy chews on the arm of the chair when he is alone, you will probably discipline him angrily when you get home. Thus, he makes the association that your coming home means he is going to be punished. (He will not remember chewing the chair and is incapable of making the association of the discipline with his naughty deed.) Accustoming the pup to his designated area not only keeps him safe but also avoids his engaging in destructive behaviors when you are not around.

HOW MANY TIMES A DAY?

AGE	RELIEF TRIPS
To 14 weeks	10
14–22 weeks	8
22–32 weeks	6
Adulthood	4
(dog stops growing)	

These are estimates, of course, but they are a guide to the *minimum* number of opportunities a dog should have each day to relieve himself.

Times of excitement, such as special occasions, family parties, etc., can be fun for the puppy, providing that he can view the activities from the security of his designated area. He is not underfoot and he is not being fed all sorts of tidbits that will probably cause him stomach distress, yet he still feels a part of the fun.

ESTABLISHING A SCHEDULE
A puppy should be taken to his relief area each time he is released from his designated area, after

Puppies quickly adjust to their crates and rarely have accidents inside them. Providing your Toy Fox Terrier puppy with a corner of his own is a positive step towards a clean life with your dog.

meals, after play sessions and when he first awakens in the morning (at age eight weeks, this can mean 5 a.m.!). The puppy will indicate that he's ready "to go" by circling or sniffing busily—do not misinterpret these signs. For a puppy less than ten weeks of age, a routine of taking him out every hour is necessary. As the puppy grows, he will be able to wait for longer periods of time.

Keep trips to his relief area short. Stay no more than five or six minutes and then return to the house. If he goes during that time, praise him lavishly and take him indoors immediately. If he does not, but he has an accident when you go back indoors, pick him up immediately, say "No! No!" and return to his relief area. Wait a few minutes, then return to the house again. Never hit a puppy or put his face in urine or excrement when he has had an accident!

Once indoors, put the puppy in his crate until you have had time to clean up his accident. Then, release him to the family area and watch him more closely than before. Chances are, his accident was a result of your not picking up his signal or waiting too long before offering him the opportunity to relieve himself. Never hold a grudge against the puppy for accidents.

Let the puppy learn that going outdoors means it is time to relieve himself, not to play. Once trained, he will be able to play indoors and out and still differentiate between the times for play versus the times for relief. Help him develop regular hours for naps, being alone, playing by himself and just resting, all in his crate. Encourage him to entertain himself while you are busy with your activities. Let him learn that having you near is comforting, but it is not your main purpose in life to provide him with undivided attention. Each time you put your puppy in his own area, use the same command, whatever suits best. Soon he will run to his crate or special area when he hears you say those words.

Crate training provides safety for you, the puppy and the home. It also provides the puppy with a feeling of security, and that helps the puppy achieve self-confidence and clean habits. Remember that one of the primary ingredients in housebreaking your puppy is control. Regardless of your lifestyle, there will always be occasions when you will need to have a place where your dog can stay and be happy and safe. Crate training is the answer for now and in the future.

In conclusion, a few key elements are really all you need for a successful housebreaking method—consistency, frequency, praise, control and supervision. By following these procedures with a normal, healthy puppy, you and the puppy will soon be past the stage of "accidents" and ready to move on to a clean and rewarding life together.

ROLES OF DISCIPLINE, REWARD AND PUNISHMENT

Discipline, training one to act in accordance with rules, brings order to life. It is as simple as that. Without discipline, particularly in a group society, chaos will reign supreme and the group will eventually perish. Humans and canines are social animals and need some form of discipline in order to function effectively. They must procure food, reproduce to keep their species going and protect their home base and their young.

If there were no discipline in the lives of social animals, they would eventually die from starvation and/or predation by other stronger animals. In the case of domestic canines, discipline in their lives is needed in order for them to understand how their pack (you and other family

FEAR AGGRESSION

Pups who are subjected to physical abuse during training commonly end up with behavioral problems as adults. One common result of abuse is fear aggression, in which a dog will lash out, bare his teeth, snarl and finally bite someone by whom he feels threatened. For example, your daughter may be playing with the dog one afternoon. As they play hide-and-seek, she backs the dog into a corner and, as she attempts to tease him playfully, he bites her hand. Examine the cause of this behavior. Did your daughter ever hit the dog? Did someone who resembles your daughter hit or scream at the dog?

Fortunately, fear aggression is relatively easy to correct. Have your daughter engage in only positive activities with the dog, such as feeding, petting and walking. She should not give any corrections or negative feedback. If the dog still growls or cowers away from her, allow someone else to accompany them. After approximately one week, the dog should feel that he can rely on her for many positive things, and he will also be prevented from reacting fearfully towards anyone who might resemble her.

COMMAND STANCE

Stand up straight and authoritatively when giving your dog commands. Do not issue commands when lying on the floor or lying on your back on the sofa. If you are on your hands and knees when you give a command, your dog will think you are positioning yourself to play.

members) functions and how they must act in order to survive.

A large humane society in a highly populated area recently surveyed dog owners regarding their satisfaction with their relationships with their dogs. People who had trained their dogs were 75% more satisfied with their pets than those who had never trained their dogs.

Dr. Edward Thorndike, a noted psychologist, established *Thorndike's Theory of Learning*, which states that a behavior that results in a pleasant event tends to be repeated. Furthermore, it concludes that a behavior that results in an unpleasant event tends not to be repeated. It is this theory upon which training methods are based today. For example, if you manipulate a dog to perform a specific behavior and reward him for doing it, he is likely to do it again because he enjoyed the end result.

Occasionally, punishment, a penalty inflicted for an offense, is necessary. The best type of punishment often comes from an outside source. For example, a child is told not to touch the stove because he may get burned. He disobeys and touches the stove. In doing so, he receives a burn. From that time on, he respects the heat of the stove and avoids contact with it. Therefore, a behavior that results in an unpleasant event tends not to be repeated.

All dogs welcome structure in their lives, including the Toy Fox Terriers. This breeder is using exercise pens inside the home to give the Toy Fox "pack" structured time for exercise and activity.

A good example of a dog learning the hard way is the dog who chases the house cat. He is told many times to leave the cat alone, yet he persists in teasing the cat. Then, one day, the dog begins chasing the cat but the cat turns and swipes a claw across the dog's face, leaving the dog with a painful gash on his nose. The final result is that the dog stops chasing the cat.

TRAINING EQUIPMENT

COLLAR AND LEASH
For a Toy Fox Terrier, the collar and leash that you use for training must be one with which you are easily able to work, not too heavy for the dog and perfectly safe.

TREATS
Have a bag of treats on hand; something nutritious and easy to swallow works best. Use a soft treat, a chunk of cheese or a piece of cooked chicken rather than a dry biscuit. By the time the dog has finished chewing a dry treat, he will forget why he is being rewarded in the first place!

Incidentally, using food rewards will not teach a dog to beg at the table—the only way to teach a dog to beg at the table is to give him food from the table. In training, rewarding the dog with a food treat will help him associate praise and the treats with learning new behaviors that obviously please his owner.

Do not go directly to him, but stop about a foot short of him and hold out the treat as you ask "School?" He will see you approaching with a treat in your hand and most likely begin walking toward you. As you meet, give him the treat and praise again.

The third time, ask the question, have a treat in your hand and walk only a short distance toward the dog so that he must walk almost all the way to you. As he reaches you, give him the treat and praise again.

By this time, the dog will probably be getting the idea that if he pays attention to you, especially when you ask that question, it will pay off in treats and enjoyable activities for him. In other words, he learns that "school" means doing great things with you that are fun and that result in positive attention for him.

Remember that the dog does not understand your verbal language; he only recognizes sounds. Your question translates to a series of sounds for him, and those sounds become the signal to go to you and pay attention. The dog learns that if he does this, he will get to interact with you plus receive treats and praise.

TRAINING BEGINS: ASK THE DOG A QUESTION

In order to teach your dog anything, you must first get his attention. After all, he cannot learn anything if he is looking away from you with his mind on something else.

To get your dog's attention, ask him "School?" and immediately walk over to him and give him a treat as you tell him "Good dog." Wait a minute or two and repeat the routine, this time with a treat in your hand as you approach within a foot of the dog.

THE BASIC COMMANDS

TEACHING SIT

Now that you have the dog's attention, attach his leash and

hold it in your left hand, and hold a food treat in your right hand. Place your food hand at the dog's nose and let him lick the treat but not take it from you. Say "Sit" and slowly raise your food hand from in front of the dog's nose up over his head so that he is looking at the ceiling. As he bends his head upward, he will have to bend his knees to maintain his balance. As he bends his knees, he will assume a sit position. At that point, release the food treat and praise lavishly with comments such as "Good dog! Good sit!," etc. Remember to always praise enthusiastically, because dogs relish verbal praise from their owners and feel so proud of themselves whenever they accomplish a behavior.

You will not use food forever in getting the dog to obey your commands. Food is only used to teach new behaviors and, once the dog knows what you want when you give a specific command, you will wean him off the food treats but still maintain the verbal praise. After all, you will always have your voice with you, and there will be many times when you have no food rewards but expect the dog to obey.

TEACHING DOWN

Teaching the down exercise is easy when you understand how the dog perceives the down position, and it is very difficult when

SAFETY FIRST

While it may seem that the most important things to your dog are eating, sleeping and chewing the upholstery on your furniture, his first concern is actually safety. The domesticated dogs we keep as companions have the same pack instinct as their ancestors who ran free thousands of years ago. Because of this pack instinct, your dog wants to know that he and his pack are not in danger of being harmed, and that his pack has a strong, capable leader. You must establish yourself as the leader early on in your relationship. That way your dog will trust that you will take care of him and the pack, and he will accept your commands without question.

you do not. Dogs perceive the down position as a submissive one; therefore, teaching the down exercise by using a forceful method can sometimes make the dog develop such a fear of the down that he either runs away when you say "Down" or he attempts to snap at the person who tries to force him down.

Have the dog sit close alongside your left leg, facing in the same direction as you are. Hold the leash in your left hand and a food treat in your right. Now place your left hand lightly on the top of the dog's shoulders where they meet above the spinal cord. Do not push down on the dog's shoulders; simply rest your left hand there so you can guide the dog to lie down close to your left leg rather than to swing away from your side when he drops.

The down and down/stay commands require that the Toy Fox Terrier feel completely comfortable with his trainer and his surroundings.

Now place the food hand at the dog's nose, say "Down" very softly (almost a whisper) and slowly lower the food hand to the dog's front feet. When the food hand reaches the floor, begin moving it forward along the floor in front of the dog. Keep talking softly to the dog, saying things like, "Do you want this treat? You can do this, good dog." Your reassuring tone of voice will help calm the dog as he tries to follow the food hand in order to get the treat.

When the dog's elbows touch the floor, release the food and praise softly. Try to get the dog to maintain that down position for several seconds before you let him sit up again. The goal here is to get the dog to settle down and not feel threatened in the down position.

TEACHING STAY

It is easy to teach the dog to stay in either a sit or a down position. Again, we use food and praise during the teaching process as we help the dog to understand exactly what it is that we are expecting him to do.

To teach the sit/stay, start with the dog sitting on your left side as before and hold the leash in your left hand. Have a food treat in your right hand and place your food hand at the dog's nose. Say "Stay" and step out on your right foot to stand directly in front of the dog, toe to toe, as he licks and nibbles the treat. Be sure to keep his head facing upward to maintain the sit position. Count to five and then swing around to stand next to the dog again with him on your left. As soon as you get back to the original position, release the food and praise lavishly.

To teach the down/stay, do the down as previously described. As soon as the dog lies down, say "Stay" and step out on your right foot just as you did in the sit/stay. Count to five and then return to stand beside the dog with him on your left side. Release the treat and praise as always.

Within a week or ten days, you can begin to add a bit of distance between you and your dog when you leave him. When you do, use your left hand open with the palm facing the dog as a stay signal, much the same as the hand signal a police officer uses to stop traffic at an intersection. Hold the food treat in your right hand as before, but this time the food

Begin with the sit command, as this is the simplest of commands that you will teach your Toy Fox Terrier and a basis for further exercises.

will not be touching the dog's nose. He will watch the food hand and quickly learn that he is going to get that treat as soon as you return to his side.

When you can stand 3 feet away from your dog for 30 seconds, you can then begin building time and distance in both stays. Eventually, the dog can be expected to remain in the stay position for prolonged periods of time until you return to him or call him to you. Always praise lavishly when he stays.

TEACHING COME

If you make teaching "come" an exciting experience, you should never have a "student" that does not love the game or that fails to come when called. The secret, it seems, is never to teach the word "come."

At times when an owner most wants his dog to come when called, the owner is likely to be upset or anxious and he allows these feelings to come through in the tone of his voice when he calls his dog. Hearing that desperation in his owner's voice, the dog fears the results of going to him and therefore either disobeys outright or runs in the opposite direction. The secret, therefore, is to teach the dog a game and, when you want him to come to you, simply play the game. It is practically a no-fail solution!

To begin, have several members of your family take a few food treats and each go into a different room in the house. Everyone takes turns calling the dog, and each person should celebrate the dog's finding him with a treat and lots of happy praise. When a person calls the dog, he is actually inviting the dog to find him and to get a treat as a reward for "winning."

CONSISTENCY PAYS OFF

Dogs need consistency in their feeding schedule, exercise and relief visits, and in the verbal commands you use. If you use "Stay" on Monday and "Stay here, please" on Tuesday, you will confuse your dog. Don't demand perfect behavior during training sessions and then let him have the run of the house the rest of the day. Above all, lavish praise on your pet consistently every time he does something right. The more he feels he is pleasing you, the more willing he will be to learn.

A few turns of the "Where are you?" game and the dog will understand that everyone is playing the game and that each person has a big celebration awaiting the dog's success at locating him or her. Once the dog learns to love the game, simply calling out "Where are you?" will bring him running from wherever he is when he hears that all-important question.

The come command is recognized as one of the most important things to teach a dog, but there are trainers who work with thousands of dogs and never use the actual word "come." Yet these dogs will race to respond to a person who uses the dog's name followed by "Where are you?" For example, a woman has a 12-year-old companion dog who went blind, but who never fails to locate her owner when asked, "Where are you?"

Children, in particular, love to play this game with their dogs. Children can hide in smaller places like a shower stall or bathtub, behind a bed or under a table. The dog needs to work a little bit harder to find these hiding places, but, when he does, he loves to celebrate with a treat and a tussle with a favorite youngster.

TEACHING HEEL

Heeling means that the dog walks beside the owner without pulling. It takes time and patience on the

"Where are you?" always works better for the recall than commanding "Come" when you are upset or anxious.

owner's part to succeed at teaching the dog that he (the owner) will not proceed unless the dog is walking calmly beside him. Neither pulling out ahead on the leash nor lagging behind is acceptable.

Begin by holding the leash in your left hand as the dog sits beside your left leg. Move the loop end of the leash to your right hand, but keep your left hand short on the leash so that it keeps the dog in close next to you.

"COME" ... BACK

Never call your dog to come to you for a correction or scold him when he reaches you. That is the quickest way to turn a come command into "Go away fast!" Dogs think only in the present tense, and your dog will connect the scolding with coming to you, not with the misbehavior of a few moments earlier.

Do not engage in a battle of wills with your "non-heeling" Toy Fox Terrier. Pulling on the leash will not convince the dog, and he will likely pull back! Simply stand your ground and let the dog realize that you are the stronger, larger boss in charge.

Say "Heel" and step forward on your left foot. Keep the dog close to you and take three steps. Stop and have the dog sit next to you in what we now call the heel position. Praise verbally, but do not touch the dog. Hesitate a moment and begin again with "Heel," taking three steps and stopping, at which point the dog is told to sit again.

Your goal here is to have the dog walk those three steps without pulling on the leash. Once he will walk calmly beside you for three steps without pulling, increase the number of steps you take to five. When he will walk politely beside you while you take five steps, you can increase the length of your walk to ten steps. Keep increasing the length of your stroll until the dog will walk quietly beside you without

pulling as long as you want him to heel. When you stop heeling, indicate to the dog that the exercise is over by verbally praising as you pet him and say "OK, good dog." The "OK" is used as a release word, meaning that the exercise is finished and the dog is free to relax.

If you are dealing with a dog who insists on pulling you around, simply "put on your brakes" and stand your ground until the dog realizes that the two of you are not going anywhere until he is beside you and moving at your pace, not his. It may take some time just standing there to convince the dog that you are the leader and that you will be the one to decide on the direction and speed of your travel.

Each time the dog looks up at you or slows down to give a slack leash between the two of you, quietly praise him and say, "Good heel. Good dog." Eventually, the dog will begin to respond and within a few days he will be walking politely beside you without pulling on the leash. At first, the training sessions should be kept short and very positive; soon the dog will be able to walk nicely with you for increasingly longer distances. Remember also to give the dog free time and the opportunity to run and play when you have finished heel practice.

WEANING OFF FOOD IN TRAINING

Food is used in training new behaviors. Once the dog understands what behavior goes with a specific command, it is time to start weaning him off the food treats. At first, give a treat after each exercise. Then, start to give a treat only after every other exercise. Mix up the times when you offer a food reward and the times when you only offer praise so that the dog will never know when he is going to receive both food and praise and when he is going to receive only praise. This is called a variable-ratio reward system. It proves successful because there is always the chance that the owner will produce a treat, so the dog never stops trying for that reward. No matter what, *always* give verbal praise.

OBEDIENCE CLASSES

It is a good idea to enroll in an obedience class if one is available in your area. If yours is a show dog, classes to prepare the dog for the show ring would be more appropriate. Many areas have dog clubs that offer basic obedience training as well as preparatory classes for obedience competition. There are also local dog trainers who offer similar classes.

At obedience trials, dogs can earn titles at various levels of competition, and the Toy Fox Terrier is an enthusiastic competitor. The beginning levels of obedience competition include basic behaviors such as sit, down, heel, etc. The more advanced levels of competition include jumping, retrieving, scent discrimination and signal work. The advanced levels require a dog and owner to put a lot of time and effort into their training. The titles that can be earned at these levels of competition are very prestigious.

OTHER ACTIVITIES FOR LIFE

Whether a dog is trained in the structured environment of a class or alone with his owner at

---

HOW TO WEAN THE "TREAT HOG"

If you have trained your dog by rewarding him with a treat each time he performs a command, he may soon decide that without the treat, he won't sit, stay or come. The best way to fix this problem is to start asking your dog to do certain commands twice before being rewarded. Slowly increase the number of commands given and then vary the number: three sits and a treat one day, five sits for a biscuit the next day, etc. Your dog will soon realize that there is no set number of sits before he gets his reward and he'll likely do it the first time you ask in the hope of being rewarded sooner rather than later.

Such a large obstacle is no problem for the diminutive Toy Fox. With dexterity and grace, this dog is managing the A-frame at an agility trial.

by occupying his mind and providing an outlet for his energy.

Backpacking is an exciting and healthy activity that the dog can be taught without assistance from more than his owner. The exercise of walking and climbing is good for man and dog alike, and the bond that they develop together is priceless. The rule for backpacking with any dog is never to expect the dog to carry more than one-sixth of his body weight; for the Toy Fox, this will not be much, so the focus in hiking is on the actual walk, not on the dog's carrying a pack.

home, there are many activities that can bring fun and rewards to both owner and dog once they have mastered basic control. Toy Fox Terriers are especially adaptive for Assistance Dog and Hearing Ear programs for the deaf. They also make excellent therapy dogs for hospitals and homes for the elderly. In addition, the larger representatives of the breed have proven to be good hunters, while even the smallest are excellent as "mousers."

Teaching the dog to help out around the home, in the yard or on the farm provides great satisfaction to both dog and owner. In addition, the dog's help makes life a little easier for his owner and raises his stature as a valued companion to his family. It helps give the dog a purpose

If you are interested in participating in organized competition with your Toy Fox Terrier, there are activities other than obedience in which you and your dog can become involved. Agility is a popular sport in which dogs run through an obstacle course that includes various jumps, tunnels and other exercises to test the dog's speed and coordination. Just as with obedience competition, the Toy Fox shows great enthusiasm for and great skill at agility.

In an agility trial, the owners run beside their dogs to give commands and to guide the dogs through the course. Although competitive, the focus is on fun—it's fun to do, fun to watch and great exercise for both dogs and handlers.

Dogs suffer from many of the same physical illnesses as people and might even share many of the same psychological problems. Since people usually know more about human diseases than canine maladies, many of the terms used in this chapter will be familiar but not necessarily those used by veterinarians. For example, we will use the familiar term *x-ray* instead of *radiograph*. We will also use the familiar term *symptoms*, even though dogs don't have symptoms, which are verbal descriptions of something the patient feels or observes himself that he regards as abnormal. Dogs have *clinical signs* since they cannot speak, so we have to look for these clinical signs...but we still use the term *symptoms* in the book.

Medicine is a constantly changing art, with of course scientific input as well. Things alter as we learn more and more about basic sciences such as genetics and biochemistry, and have use of more sophisticated imaging techniques like Computer Aided Tomography (CAT scans) or Magnetic Resonance Imaging (MRI scans). There is academic dispute about many canine maladies, so different veterinarians treat them in different ways; for example, some vets place a greater emphasis on surgical treatment options than others.

SELECTING A VETERINARIAN

Your selection of a veterinarian should be based on personal recommendation for his skills with dogs, and, if possible, especially toy breeds. It's even better if the vet has experience with the Toy Fox Terrier in particular. If the vet is based nearby, it will be helpful because you might have an emergency or need to make

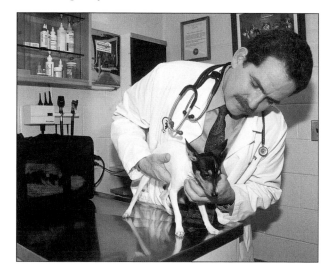

Your Toy Fox Terrier's veterinarian should be knowledgeable about small dogs as well as able to communicate with you about your dog's health care.

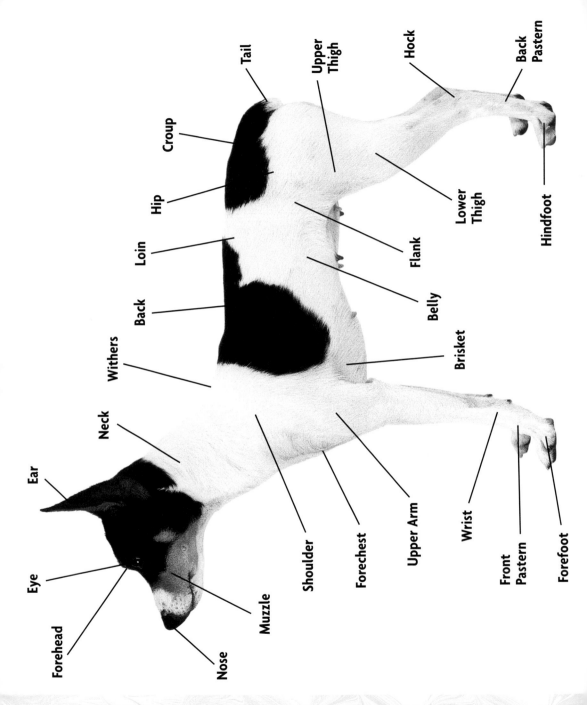

PHYSICAL STRUCTURE OF THE TOY FOX TERRIER

multiple visits for treatments.

All veterinarians are licensed and capable of dealing with routine medical issues such as infections, injuries and the promotion of health (for example, by vaccination). Most vets do routine surgery such as neutering, stitching up wounds and docking tails in breeds for which such is required for show purposes.

If the problem affecting your dog is more complex, your vet will refer your pet to someone with a more detailed knowledge of what is wrong. This will usually be a specialist, perhaps at the nearest university veterinary school, who concentrates in the field relevant to your dog's problem (veterinary dermatology, veterinary ophthalmology, etc.).

Veterinary procedures are very costly and, as the treatments available improve, they are going to become more expensive. It is quite acceptable to discuss matters of cost with your vet; if there is more than one treatment option, cost may be a factor in deciding which route to take. It also is not impudent to get a second opinion, although it is courteous to advise the vets concerned that you are doing so.

Just as humans have health insurance, insurance against veterinary cost is becoming very popular. Most policies cover illnesses and emergencies such as accidents; more extensive policies

Breakdown of Veterinary Income by Category

2%	**Dentistry**
4%	**Radiology**
12%	**Surgery**
15%	**Vaccinations**
19%	**Laboratory**
23%	**Examinations**
25%	**Medicines**

A typical vet's income, categorized according to services performed. This survey dealt with small-animal (pets) practices.

cover routine care, including yearly check-ups, prescription flea control and vaccinations.

PREVENTATIVE MEDICINE

It is much easier, less costly and more effective to practice preventative medicine than to fight bouts of illness and disease. Properly bred puppies of all breeds come from parents that were selected based upon their genetic-disease profiles. The puppies' mother should have been vaccinated, free of all internal and external parasites and properly nourished. For these reasons, a visit to the veterinarian who cared for the dam is recommended if at all possible. The dam passes disease resistance to her puppies, which should last from eight to ten weeks. Unfortunately, she can also pass on parasites and infection. This is why

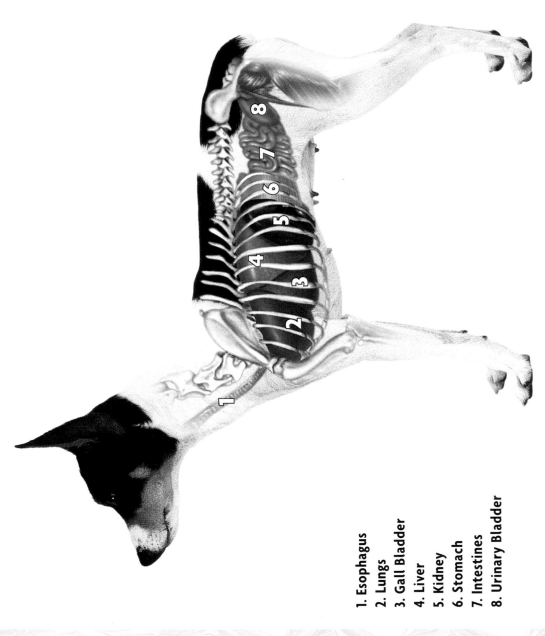

1. Esophagus
2. Lungs
3. Gall Bladder
4. Liver
5. Kidney
6. Stomach
7. Intestines
8. Urinary Bladder

INTERNAL ORGANS OF THE TOY FOX TERRIER

knowledge about her health is useful in learning more about the health of the puppies.

WEANING TO FIVE MONTHS OLD
Puppies should be weaned by the time they are two months old. A puppy that remains for at least eight weeks with his mother and litter-mates usually adapts better to other dogs and people later in life.

Sometimes new owners have their puppy examined by a vet immediately, which is a good idea unless the puppy is overtired by a long journey home from the breeder's. In that case, the appoint-

ment should be arranged for within a day or two of bringing the pup home.

The puppy will have his teeth examined and have his skeletal conformation and general health checked prior to certification by the veterinarian. Puppies in certain breeds have problems with their kneecaps, cataracts and other eye problems, heart murmurs and undescended testicles. Your veterinarian might have training in temperament evaluation and be able to give you advice about your youngster's personality. Also at the first visit, the vet will set up a schedule for the pup's vaccinations.

HEALTH AND VACCINATION SCHEDULE

AGE IN WEEKS:	6TH	8TH	10TH	12TH	14TH	16TH	20-24TH	52ND
Worm Control	✔	✔	✔	✔	✔	✔	✔	
Neutering							✔	
Heartworm		✔		✔		✔	✔	
Parvovirus	✔		✔		✔		✔	✔
Distemper		✔		✔		✔		✔
Hepatitis		✔		✔		✔		✔
Leptospirosis								✔
Parainfluenza	✔		✔		✔			✔
Dental Examination		✔					✔	✔
Complete Physical		✔					✔	✔
Coronavirus				✔			✔	✔
Canine Cough	✔							
Hip Dysplasia								✔
Rabies							✔	

Vaccinations are not instantly effective. It takes about two weeks for the dog's immune system to develop antibodies. Most vaccinations require annual booster shots. Your vet should guide you in this regard.

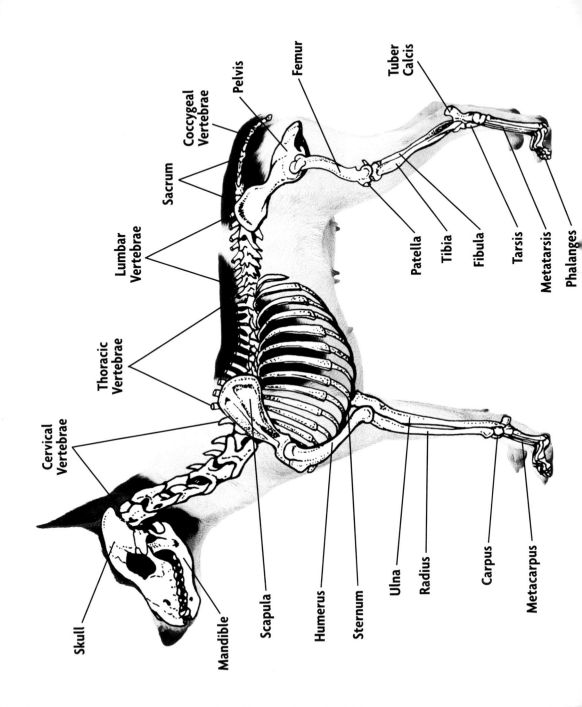

SKELETAL STRUCTURE OF THE TOY FOX TERRIER

VACCINATIONS

Most vaccinations are given by injection and should only be given by a veterinarian. Both he and you should keep a record of the date of the injection, the identification of the vaccine and the amount given. Some vets give a first vaccination at around six weeks, but some dog breeders prefer the course not to commence until about eight weeks because of the risk of interaction with the antibodies produced by the mother. This varies from pup to pup, based on the individual's immunity level.

The vaccination schedule is usually based on a two- to four-week cycle. You must take your vet's advice as to when to vaccinate, as this may differ according to the vaccine used.

The usual vaccines contain immunizing doses of several different viruses such as distemper, parvovirus, parainfluenza and hepatitis. There are other vaccines available when the puppy is at risk. You should rely upon professional advice. This is especially true for the booster immunizations. Most vaccination programs require a booster when

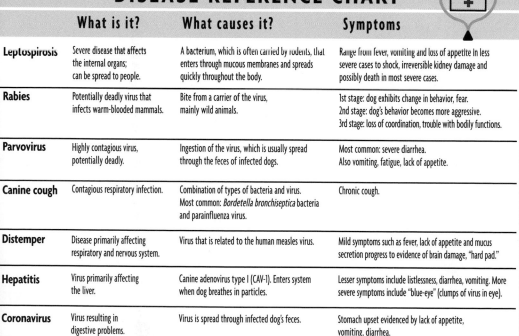

DISEASE REFERENCE CHART

	What is it?	What causes it?	Symptoms
Leptospirosis	Severe disease that affects the internal organs; can be spread to people.	A bacterium, which is often carried by rodents, that enters through mucous membranes and spreads quickly throughout the body.	Range from fever, vomiting and loss of appetite in less severe cases to shock, irreversible kidney damage and possibly death in most severe cases.
Rabies	Potentially deadly virus that infects warm-blooded mammals.	Bite from a carrier of the virus, mainly wild animals.	1st stage: dog exhibits change in behavior, fear. 2nd stage: dog's behavior becomes more aggressive. 3rd stage: loss of coordination, trouble with bodily functions.
Parvovirus	Highly contagious virus, potentially deadly.	Ingestion of the virus, which is usually spread through the feces of infected dogs.	Most common: severe diarrhea. Also vomiting, fatigue, lack of appetite.
Canine cough	Contagious respiratory infection.	Combination of types of bacteria and virus. Most common: *Bordetella bronchiseptica* bacteria and parainfluenza virus.	Chronic cough.
Distemper	Disease primarily affecting respiratory and nervous system.	Virus that is related to the human measles virus.	Mild symptoms such as fever, lack of appetite and mucus secretion progress to evidence of brain damage, "hard pad."
Hepatitis	Virus primarily affecting the liver.	Canine adenovirus type I (CAV-1). Enters system when dog breathes in particles.	Lesser symptoms include listlessness, diarrhea, vomiting. More severe symptoms include "blue-eye" (clumps of virus in eye).
Coronavirus	Virus resulting in digestive problems.	Virus is spread through infected dog's feces.	Stomach upset evidenced by lack of appetite, vomiting, diarrhea.

the puppy is a year old and once a year thereafter. In some cases, circumstances may require more or less frequent immunizations.

Canine cough, more formally known as tracheobronchitis, is immunized against with a vaccine that is sprayed into the dog's nostrils. Canine cough is usually included in routine vaccination, but it is often not as effective as the vaccines for other major diseases.

FIVE MONTHS TO ONE YEAR OF AGE
Unless you intend to breed or show your dog, neutering the puppy at the appropriate age is advised, and likely will have been required by the breeder when you purchased your pup. Opinions vary regarding the best age at which to have this procedure done (usually around six months), so discuss all aspects with your veterinarian. Neutering males and spaying females have proven to be extremely beneficial. Besides eliminating the possibility of pregnancy, it inhibits (but does not prevent) breast cancer in bitches and prostate cancer in male dogs.

Your veterinarian should

Normal hairs of a dog enlarged 200 times original size. The cuticle (outer covering) is clean and healthy. Unlike human hair that grows from the base, a dog's hair also grows from the end. Damaged hairs and split ends, illustrated above.

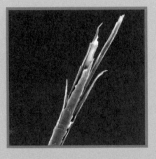
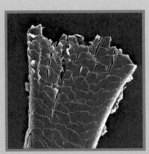
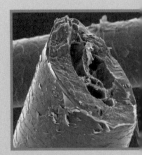

provide your puppy with a thorough dental evaluation at six months of age, ascertaining whether all of the permanent teeth have erupted properly. A home dental-care regimen should be initiated at six months, including brushing weekly and providing good dental devices (such as hard plastic or nylon bones). Regular dental care promotes healthy teeth, fresh breath and a longer life.

Dogs Older than One Year
Continue to visit the veterinarian at least once a year. There is no such disease as "old age," but bodily functions do change with age. The eyes and ears are no longer as efficient. Liver, kidney and intestinal functions often decline. Proper dietary changes, recommended by your veterinarian, can make life more pleasant for your aging Toy Fox Terrier and you.

SKIN PROBLEMS
Veterinarians are consulted by dog owners for skin problems more than for any other group of diseases or maladies. A dog's skin is as sensitive, if not more so, than human skin, and both suffer from almost the same ailments (though the occurrence of acne in most breeds is rare). For this reason, veterinary dermatology has developed into a specialty practiced by many veterinarians.

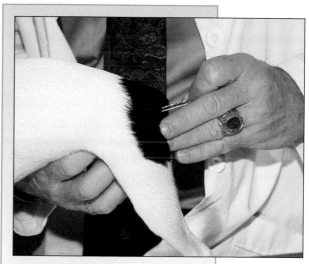

VITAL SIGNS
A dog's normal temperature is 101.5 degrees Fahrenheit. A range of between 100.0 and 102.5 degrees should be considered normal, as each dog's body sets its own temperature. It will be helpful if you take your dog's temperature when you know he is healthy and record it. Then, when you suspect that he is not feeling well, you will have a normal figure to compare the abnormal temperature against.

The normal pulse rate for a dog is between 100 and 125 beats per minute.

Since many skin problems have visual symptoms that are almost identical, it requires the skill of an experienced veterinary dermatologist to identify and cure many of the more severe skin disorders. Pet shops sell many treatments for skin problems, but most of the treat-

meaning that they carry, but are not affected by, the disease. These diseases pose serious problems to breeders because in some instances there are no methods of identifying carriers. Often the secondary diseases associated with these skin conditions are even more debilitating than the skin disorders themselves, including cancers and respiratory problems.

Among the hereditary skin disorders, for which the mode of inheritance is known, are acrodermatitis, cutaneous asthenia (Ehlers-Danlos syndrome), sebaceous adenitis, cyclic hematopoiesis, dermatomyositis, IgA deficiency, color dilution alopecia and nodular dermatofibrosis. Some of these disorders are limited to one or two breeds, while others affect a large number of breeds. All inherited diseases must be diagnosed and treated by a veterinary specialist.

Parasite Bites

Many of us are allergic to insect bites. The bites itch, erupt and may even become infected. Dogs have the same reaction to fleas, ticks and/or mites. When an insect lands on you, you have the chance to whisk it away with your hand. Unfortunately, when a dog is bitten by a flea, tick or mite, he can only scratch it away or bite it. By the time the dog has been bitten, the parasite has done

Your Toy Fox Terrier will enjoy time outdoors, but be sure to check his coat after he returns inside for signs of insect bites, grass allergies and other irritants.

ments are directed at symptoms and not at the underlying problem(s). If your dog is suffering from a skin disorder, you should seek professional assistance as quickly as possible. As with all diseases, the earlier a problem is identified and treated, the more successful can be the cure.

Hereditary Skin Disorders

Veterinary dermatologists are currently researching a number of skin disorders that are believed to have a hereditary basis. These inherited diseases are transmitted by both parents, who appear (phenotypically) normal but have a recessive gene for the disease, some of its damage. It may also have laid eggs, which will cause further problems in the near future. The itching from parasite bites is probably due to the saliva injected into the site when the parasite sucks the dog's blood.

AIRBORNE ALLERGIES

Just as humans suffer from hay fever during the pollinating season, many dogs suffer from the same allergies. When the pollen count is high, your dog might suffer, but don't expect him to sneeze and have a runny nose as a human would. Dogs react to pollen allergies in the same way they react to fleas—they scratch and bite themselves. Dogs, like humans, can be tested for allergens. Discuss the testing with your veterinarian.

KNOW WHEN TO POSTPONE A VACCINATION

While the visit to the vet is costly, it is never advisable to update a vaccination when visiting with a sick or pregnant dog. Vaccinations should be avoided for all elderly dogs. If your dog is showing the signs of any illness or any medical condition, no matter how serious or mild, including skin irritations, do not vaccinate. Likewise, a lame dog should never be vaccinated; any dog undergoing surgery or on any immunosuppressant drugs also should not be vaccinated until fully recovered.

AUTO-IMMUNE ILLNESSES

An auto-immune illness is one in which the immune system over-acts and does not recognize parts of the affected person; rather, the immune system starts to react as if these parts were foreign and need to be destroyed. An example is rheumatoid arthritis, which occurs when the body does not recognize the joints, thus leading to a very painful and damaging reaction in the joints. This has nothing to do with age, so can occur in children and young dogs. The wear-and-tear arthritis of the older person or dog is osteoarthritis.

Lupus is an auto-immune disease that affects dogs as well as people. It can take variable forms, affecting the kidneys, bones and the skin. It can be fatal, so is treated with steroids, which can themselves have very significant side effects. The steroids calm down the allergic reaction to the body's tissues, which helps the lupus, but steroids decrease the body's reaction to real foreign substances such as bacteria, and steroids also thin the skin and bones.

FOOD PROBLEMS

FOOD ALLERGIES

Some dogs can be allergic to many foods that may be best-sellers and highly recommended by breeders and veterinarians.

Changing the brand of food that you buy may not eliminate the problem if the element to which the dog is allergic is contained in the new brand.

Recognizing a food allergy in a dog can be difficult. Humans often have rashes when they eat foods to which they are allergic, or have swelling of the lips or eyes. Dogs do not usually develop rashes, but react in the same way as they do to an airborne or bite allergy—they itch, scratch and bite. While pollen allergies are usually seasonal, food allergies are year-round problems.

TREATING FOOD ALLERGY

Diagnosis of food allergy is based on a two- to four-week dietary trial with a home-cooked diet fed to the exclusion of all other foods. The diet should consist of boiled rice or potato with a source of protein that the dog has never eaten before, such as fresh or frozen fish, lamb or even something as exotic as pheasant. Water has to be the only drink, and it is

really important that no other foods are fed during this trial. If the dog's condition improves, you will need to try the original diet once again to see if the itching resumes. If it does, then this confirms the diagnosis that the dog is allergic to his original diet. The treatment is long-term feeding of something that does not distress the dog's skin, which may be in the form of one of the commercially available hypoallergenic diets or the home-made diet that you created for the allergy trial.

FOOD INTOLERANCE

Food intolerance is the inability of the dog to completely digest certain foods. This occurs because the dog does not have the chemicals necessary to digest some foodstuffs. These chemicals are called enzymes. All puppies have the enzymes necessary to digest canine milk, but some dogs do not have the enzymes to digest a very different form of milk that is commonly found in human households—milk from cows. In such dogs, drinking cows' milk results in loose bowels, stomach pains and the passage of gas.

Dogs often do not have the enzymes to digest soy or other beans. The treatment is to exclude the foodstuffs that upset your Toy Fox Terrier's digestion.

Number-One Killer Disease in Dogs: CANCER

In every age, there is a word associated with a disease or plague that causes humans to shudder. In the 21st century, that word is "cancer." Just as cancer is the leading cause of death in humans, it claims nearly half the lives of dogs that die from a natural disease as well as half the dogs that die over the age of ten years.

Described as a genetic disease, cancer becomes a greater risk as the dog ages. Vets and dog owners have become increasingly aware of the threat of cancer to dogs. Statistics reveal that one dog in every five will develop cancer, the most common of which is skin cancer. Many cancers, including prostate, ovarian and breast cancer, can be avoided by spaying and neutering our dogs around the age of six months.

Early detection of cancer can save or extend a dog's life, so it is absolutely vital for owners to have their dogs examined by a qualified vet or oncologist immediately upon detection of any abnormality. Certain dietary guidelines have also proven to reduce the onset and spread of cancer. Foods based on fish rather than beef, due to the presence of Omega-3 fatty acids, are recommended. Other amino acids such as glutamine have significant benefits for canines, particularly those breeds that show a greater susceptibility to cancer.

Cancer management and treatments promise hope for future generations of canines. Since the disease is genetic, breeders should never breed a dog whose parents, grandparents and any related siblings have developed cancer. It is difficult to know whether to exclude an otherwise healthy dog from a breeding program as the disease does not manifest itself until the dog's senior years.

RECOGNIZE CANCER WARNING SIGNS

Since early detection can possibly rescue your dog from becoming a cancer statistic, it is essential for owners to recognize the possible signs and seek the assistance of a qualified professional.

- Abnormal bumps or lumps that continue to grow
- Bleeding or discharge from any body cavity
- Persistent stiffness or lameness
- Recurrent sores or sores that do not heal
- Inappetence
- Breathing difficulties
- Weight loss
- Bad breath or odors
- General malaise and fatigue
- Eating and swallowing problems
- Difficulty urinating and defecating

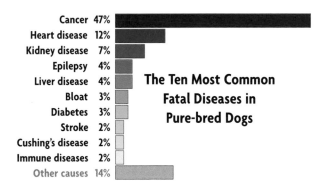

Cancer	47%
Heart disease	12%
Kidney disease	7%
Epilepsy	4%
Liver disease	4%
Bloat	3%
Diabetes	3%
Stroke	2%
Cushing's disease	2%
Immune diseases	2%
Other causes	14%

The Ten Most Common Fatal Diseases in Pure-bred Dogs

A male dog flea, *Ctenocephalides canis.*

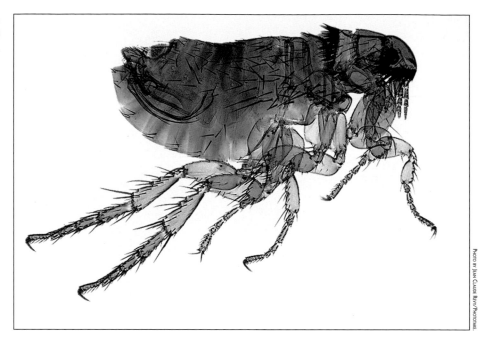

PHOTO BY JEAN CLAUDE REVY/PHOTOTAKE.

EXTERNAL PARASITES

FLEAS

Of all the problems to which dogs are prone, none is more well known and frustrating than fleas. Flea infestation is relatively simple to cure but difficult to prevent. Parasites that are harbored inside the body are a bit more difficult to eradicate but they are easier to control.

To control flea infestation, you have to understand the flea's life cycle. Fleas are often thought of as a summertime problem, but centrally heated homes have changed the patterns and fleas can be found at any time of the year. The most effective method of flea control is a two-stage approach: one stage to kill the adult fleas, and the other to control the development of pre-adult fleas. Unfortunately, no single active ingredient is effective against all stages of the life cycle.

FLEA KILLER CAUTION— "POISON"

Flea-killers are poisonous. You should not spray these toxic chemicals on areas of a dog's body that he licks, including his genitals and his face. Flea killers taken internally are a better answer, but check with your vet in case internal therapy is not advised for your dog.

LIFE CYCLE STAGES

During its life, a flea will pass through four life stages: egg, larva, pupa or nymph and adult. The adult stage is the most visible and irritating stage of the flea life cycle, and this is why the majority of flea-control products concentrate on this stage. The fact is that adult fleas account for only 1% of the total flea population, and the other 99% exist in pre-adult stages, i.e., eggs, larvae and nymphs. The pre-adult stages are barely visible to the naked eye.

THE LIFE CYCLE OF THE FLEA

Eggs are laid on the dog, usually in quantities of about 20 or 30, several times a day. The adult female flea must have a blood meal before each egg-laying session. When first laid, the eggs will cling to the dog's hair, as the eggs are still moist. However, they will quickly dry out and fall from the dog, especially if the dog moves around or scratches. Many eggs will fall off in the dog's favorite area or an area in which he spends a lot of time, such as his bed.

Once the eggs fall from the dog onto the carpet or furniture, they will hatch into larvae. This takes from one to ten days. Larvae are not particularly mobile and will usually travel only a few inches from where they hatch. However, they do have a tendency to move away from bright light and heavy

EN GARDE:
CATCHING FLEAS OFF GUARD!
Consider the following ways to arm yourself against fleas:
- Add a small amount of pennyroyal or eucalyptus oil to your dog's bath. These natural remedies repel fleas.
- Supplement your dog's food with fresh garlic (minced or grated) and a hearty amount of brewer's yeast, both of which ward off fleas.
- Use a flea comb on your dog daily. Submerge fleas in a cup of bleach to kill them quickly.
- Confine the dog to only a few rooms to limit the spread of fleas in the home.
- Vacuum daily...and get all of the crevices! Dispose of the bag every few days until the problem is under control.
- Wash your dog's bedding daily. Cover cushions where your dog sleeps with towels, and wash the towels often.

traffic—under furniture and behind doors are common places to find high quantities of flea larvae.

The flea larvae feed on dead organic matter, including adult flea feces, until they are ready to change into adult fleas. Fleas will usually remain as larvae for around seven days. After this period, the larvae will pupate into protective pupae. While inside the pupae, the larvae will undergo metamorphosis and change into

Fleas have
been measured as
being able to
jump 300,000
times and can
jump over 150
times their
length in any
direction,
including
straight up.

adult fleas. This can take as little time as a few days, but the adult fleas can remain inside the pupae waiting to hatch for up to two years. The pupae are signaled to hatch by certain stimuli, such as physical pressure—the pupae's being stepped on, heat from an animal's lying on the pupae or increased carbon-dioxide levels and vibrations—indicating that a suitable host is available.

Once hatched, the adult flea must feed within a few days. Once the adult flea finds a host, it will not leave voluntarily. It only becomes dislodged by grooming or the host animal's scratching. The adult flea will remain on the

PHOTO BY DWIGHT R. KUHN

host for the duration of its life unless forcibly removed.

TREATING THE ENVIRONMENT AND THE DOG

Treating fleas should be a two-pronged attack. First, the environment needs to be treated; this includes carpets and furniture, especially the dog's bedding and areas underneath furniture. The environment should be treated with a household spray containing an Insect Growth Regulator (IGR) and an insecticide to kill the adult fleas. Most IGRs are effective against eggs and larvae; they actually mimic the fleas' own hormones and stop the eggs and larvae from developing into adult fleas. There are currently no treatments available to attack the pupa stage of the life cycle, so the adult insecticide is used to kill the newly hatched adult fleas before they find a host. Most IGRs are active for many months, while adult insecticides are only active for a few days.

A scanning electron micrograph of a dog or cat flea, *Ctenocephalides*, magnified more than 100x. This image has been colorized for effect.

S. E. M. BY DR DENNIS KUNKEL, UNIVERSITY OF HAWAII

THE LIFE CYCLE OF THE FLEA

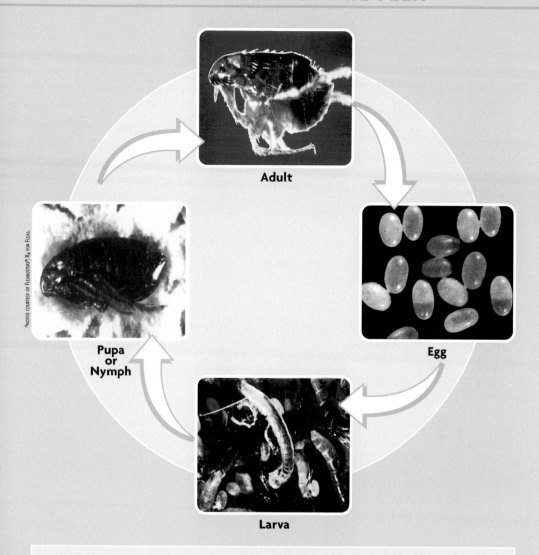

Adult

Egg

Pupa
or
Nymph

Larva

Fleas have been around for millions of years and have adapted to changing host animals. They are able to go through a complete life cycle in less than one month or they can extend their lives to almost two years by remaining as pupae or cocoons. They do not need blood or any other food for up to 20 months.

INSECT GROWTH REGULATOR (IGR)

Two types of products should be used when treating fleas—a product to treat the pet and a product to treat the home. Adult fleas represent less than 1% of the flea population. The pre-adult fleas (eggs, larvae and pupae) represent more than 99% of the flea population and are found in the environment; it is in the case of pre-adult fleas that products containing an Insect Growth Regulator (IGR) should be used in the home.

IGRs are a new class of compounds used to prevent the development of insects. They do not kill the insect outright, but instead use the insect's biology against it to stop it from completing its growth. Products that contain methoprene are the world's first and leading IGRs. Used to control fleas and other insects, this type of IGR will stop flea larvae from developing and protect the house for up to seven months.

The American dog tick, *Dermacentor variabilis*, is probably the most common tick found on dogs. Look at the strength in its eight legs! No wonder it's hard to detach them.

When treating with a household spray, it is a good idea to vacuum before applying the product. This stimulates as many pupae as possible to hatch into adult fleas. The vacuum cleaner should also be treated with an insecticide to prevent the eggs and larvae that have been collected in the vacuum bag from hatching.

The second stage of treatment is to apply an adult insecticide to the dog. Traditionally, this would be in the form of a collar or a spray, but more recent innovations include digestible insecticides that poison the fleas when they ingest the dog's blood. Alternatively, there are drops that, when placed on the back of the dog's neck, spread throughout the hair and skin to kill adult fleas.

TICKS

Though not as common as fleas, ticks are found all over the tropical and temperate world. They don't bite, like fleas; they harpoon. They dig their sharp proboscis (nose) into the dog's skin and drink the blood. Their only food and drink is dog's blood. Dogs can get Lyme

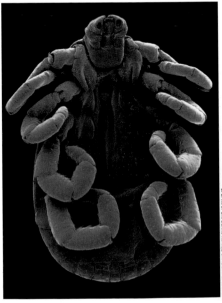

S.E.M. BY DR. DENNIS KUNKEL, UNIVERSITY OF HAWAII

disease, Rocky Mountain spotted fever, tick bite paralysis and many other diseases from ticks. They may live where fleas are found and they like to hide in cracks or seams in walls. They are controlled the same way fleas are controlled.

The American dog tick, *Dermacentor variabilis*, may well be the most common dog tick in many geographical areas, especially those areas where the climate is hot and humid. Most dog ticks have life expectancies of a week to six months, depending upon climatic conditions. They can neither jump nor fly, but they can crawl slowly and can range up to 16 feet to reach a sleeping or unsuspecting dog.

MITES

Just as fleas and ticks can be problematic for your dog, mites can also lead to an itchy nuisance. Microscopic in size, mites are related to ticks and generally take up permanent residence on their host animal—in this case, your dog! The term *mange* refers to any infestation caused by one of the mighty mites, of which there are six varieties that concern dog owners.

Demodex mites cause a condition known as demodicosis (sometimes called red mange or follicular mange), in which the

DEER-TICK CROSSING

The great outdoors may be fun for your dog, but it also is a home to dangerous ticks. Deer ticks carry a bacterium known as *Borrelia burgdorferi* and are most active in the autumn and spring. When infections are caught early, penicillin and tetracycline are effective antibiotics, but, if left untreated, the bacteria may cause neurological, kidney and cardiac problems as well as long-term trouble with walking and painful joints.

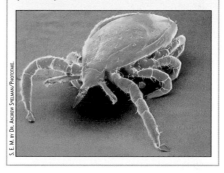

S. E. M. BY DR. ANDREW SYRED/PHOTOTAKE.

PHOTO BY DR. DENNIS KUNKEL, UNIVERSITY OF HAWAII.

The head of an American dog tick, *Dermacentor variabilis*, enlarged and colorized for effect.

mites live in the dog's hair follicles and sebaceous glands in larger-than-normal numbers. This type of mange is commonly passed from the dam to her puppies and usually shows up on the puppies' muzzles, though demodicosis is not transferable from one normal dog to another. Most dogs recover from this type of mange without any treatment, though topical therapies are commonly prescribed by the vet.

Human lice look like dog lice; the two are closely related.

The *Cheyletiellosis* mite is the hook-mouthed culprit associated with "walking dandruff," a condition that affects dogs as well as cats and rabbits. This mite lives on the surface of the animal's skin and is readily transferable through direct or indirect contact with an affected animal. The dandruff is present in the form of scaly skin, which may or may not be itchy. If not treated, this mange can affect a whole kennel of dogs and can be spread to humans as well.

The *Sarcoptes* mite causes intense itching on the dog in the form of a condition known as scabies or sarcoptic mange. The cycle of the *Sarcoptes* mite lasts about three weeks, and the mites live in the top layer of the dog's skin (epidermis), preferably in areas with little hair. Scabies is highly contagious and can be passed to humans. Sometimes an allergic reaction to the mite worsens the severe itching associated with sarcoptic mange.

Ear mites, *Otodectes cynotis,* lead to otodectic mange, which most commonly affects the outer ear canal of the dog, though other areas can be affected as well. Dogs with ear-mite infestation commonly scratch at their ears, causing further irritation, and shake their heads. Dark brown droppings in the outer ear confirm the diagnosis. Your vet can prescribe a treatment to flush out the ears and kill any eggs in the ears. A complete month of treatment is necessary to cure the mange.

Two other mites, less common in dogs, include *Dermanyssus gallinae* (the poultry or red mite) and *Eutrombicula alfreddugesi* (the North American mite associated with trombiculidiasis or chigger infestation). The poultry mite frequently lives on chickens, but can transfer to dogs who spend time near farm animals. Chigger infestation affects dogs in the Central US

DO NOT MIX
Never mix parasite-control products without first consulting your vet. Some products can become toxic when combined with others and can cause fatal consequences.

NOT A DROP TO DRINK
Never allow your dog to swim in polluted water or public areas where water quality can be suspect. Even perfectly clear water can harbor parasites, many of which can cause serious to fatal illnesses in canines. Areas inhabited by waterfowl and other wildlife are especially dangerous.

who have exposure to woodlands. The types of mange caused by both of these mites are treatable by vets.

INTERNAL PARASITES
Most animals—fishes, birds and mammals, including dogs and humans—have worms and other parasites that live inside their bodies. According to Dr. Herbert R. Axelrod, the fish pathologist, there are two kinds of parasites: dumb and smart. The smart parasites live in peaceful cooperation with their hosts (symbiosis), while the dumb parasites kill their hosts. Most worm infections are relatively easy to control. If they are not controlled, they weaken the host dog to the point that other medical problems occur, but they do not kill the host as dumb parasites would.

The brown dog tick, *Rhipicephalus sanguineus,* is an uncommon but annoying tick found on dogs.

PHOTO BY CAROLINA BIOLOGICAL SUPPLY/PHOTOTAKE

The roundworm *Rhabditis* can infect both dogs and humans.

The roundworm, *Ascaris lumbricoides*.

ROUNDWORMS

Average-size dogs can pass 1,360,000 roundworm eggs every day. For example, if there were only 1 million dogs in the world, the world would be saturated with thousands of tons of dog feces. These feces would contain around 15,000,000,000 roundworm eggs.

Up to 31% of home yards and children's sand boxes in the US contain roundworm eggs.

Flushing a dog's feces down the toilet is not a safe practice because the usual sewage treatments do not destroy roundworm eggs.

Infected puppies start shedding roundworm eggs at three weeks of age. They can be infected by their mother's milk.

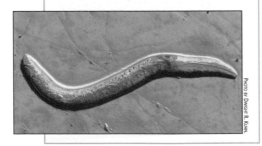

PHOTO BY DWIGHT R. KUHN

ROUNDWORMS

The roundworms that infect dogs are known scientifically as *Toxocara canis*. They live in the dog's intestines and shed eggs continually. It has been estimated that a dog produces about 6 or more ounces of feces every day. Each ounce of feces averages hundreds of thousands of roundworm eggs. There are no known areas in which dogs roam that do not contain roundworm eggs. The greatest danger of roundworms is that they infect people, too! It is wise to have your dog tested regularly for roundworms.

In young puppies, roundworms cause bloated bellies, diarrhea, coughing and vomiting, and are transmitted from the dam (through blood or milk). Affected puppies will not appear as animated as normal puppies. The worms appear spaghetti-like, measuring as long as 6 inches. Adult dogs can acquire roundworms through coprophagia (eating contaminated feces) or by killing rodents that carry roundworms.

Roundworm infection can kill puppies and cause severe problems in adults, as the hatched larvae travel to the lungs and trachea through the bloodstream. Cleanliness is the best preventative for roundworms. Always pick up after your dog and dispose of feces in appropriate receptacles.

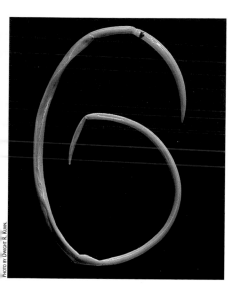

PHOTO BY DWIGHT R. KUHN.

HOOKWORMS

In the United States, dog owners have to be concerned about four different species of hookworm, the most common and most serious of which is *Ancylostoma caninum,* which prefers warm climates. The others are *Ancylostoma braziliense, Ancylostoma tubaeforme* and *Uncinaria stenocephala,* the latter of which is a concern to dogs living in the Northern US and Canada, as this species prefers cold climates. Hookworms are dangerous to humans as well as to dogs and cats, and can be the cause of severe anemia due to iron deficiency. The worm uses its teeth to attach itself to the dog's intestines and changes the site of its attachment about six times per day. Each time the worm

repositions itself, the dog loses blood and can become anemic. *Ancylostoma caninum* is the most likely of the four species to cause anemia in the dog.

Symptoms of hookworm infection include dark stools, weight loss, general weakness, pale coloration and anemia, as well as possible skin problems. Fortunately, hookworms are easily purged from affected dog with a number of medications that have proven effective. Discuss these with your vet. Most heartworm preventatives include a hookworm insecticide as well.

Owners also must be aware that hookworms can infect humans, who can acquire the larvae through exposure to contaminated feces. Since the worms cannot complete their life cycle on a human, the worms simply infest the skin and cause irritation. This condition is known as cutaneous larva migrans syndrome. As a preventative, use disposable gloves or a "poop-scoop" to pick up your dog's droppings and prevent your dog (or neighbor-hood cats) from defecating in children's play areas.

The hookworm, *Ancylostoma caninum.*

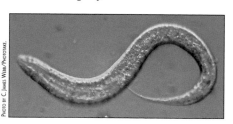

PHOTO BY C. JAMES WEBB/PHOTOTAKE.

The infective stage of the hook-worm larva.

TAPEWORMS

Humans, rats, squirrels, foxes, coyotes, wolves and domestic dogs are all susceptible to tapeworm infection. Except in humans, tapeworms are usually not a fatal infection. Infected individuals can harbor 1000 parasitic worms.

Tapeworms, like some other types of worm, are hermaphroditic, meaning male and female in the same worm.

If dogs eat infected rats or mice, or anything else infected with tapeworm, they get the tapeworm disease. One month after attaching to a dog's intestine, the worm starts shedding eggs. These eggs are infective immediately. Infective eggs can live for a few months without a host animal.

The head and rostellum (the round prominence on the scolex) of a tapeworm, which infects dogs and humans.

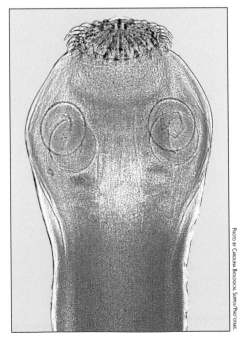

Photo by Carolina Biological Supply/Phototake.

TAPEWORMS

There are many species of tapeworm, all of which are carried by fleas! The most common tapeworm affecting dogs is known as *Dipylidium caninum*. The dog eats the flea and starts the tapeworm cycle. Humans can also be infected with tapeworms—so don't eat fleas! Fleas are so small that your dog could pass them onto your hands, your plate or your food and thus make it possible for you to ingest a flea that is carrying tapeworm eggs.

While tapeworm infection is not life-threatening in dogs (smart parasite!), it can be the cause of a very serious liver disease for humans. About 50% of the humans infected with *Echinococcus multilocularis*, a type of tapeworm that causes alveolar hydatid, perish.

WHIPWORMS

In North America, whipworms are counted among the most common parasitic worms in dogs. The whipworm's scientific name is *Trichuris vulpis*. These worms attach themselves in the lower parts of the intestine, where they feed. Affected dogs may only experience upset tummies, colic and diarrhea. These worms, however, can live for months or years in the dog, beginning their larval stage in the small intestine, spending their adult stage in the large intestine and finally passing infective eggs through the dog's feces. The only way to detect whipworms is through a fecal examination, though this is not always foolproof. Treatment for whipworms is tricky, due to the worms' unusual life-cycle pattern, and very often dogs are reinfected due to exposure to infective eggs on the ground. The whipworm eggs can survive in the environment for as long as five years; thus, cleaning up droppings in your own backyard as well as in public places is absolutely essential for sanitation purposes and the health of your dog and others.

THREADWORMS

Though less common than round-worms, hookworms and those previously mentioned, thread-worms concern dog owners in the Southwestern US and Gulf Coast area where the climate is hot and humid. Living in the small intestine of the dog, this worm measures a mere 2 millimeters and is round in shape. Like that of the whipworm, the threadworm's life cycle is very complex and the eggs and larvae are passed through the feces. A deadly disease in humans, *Strongyloides* readily infects people, and the handling of feces is the most common means of transmission. Threadworms are most often seen in young puppies; bloody diarrhea and pneumonia are symptoms. Sick puppies must be isolated and treated immediately; vets recommend a follow-up treatment one month later.

HEARTWORM PREVENTATIVES

There are many heartworm preventatives on the market, many of which are sold at your veterinarian's office. These products can be given daily or monthly, depending on the manufacturer's instructions. All of these preventatives contain chemical insecticides directed at killing heartworms, which leads to some controversy among dog owners. In effect, heartworm preventatives are necessary evils, though you should determine how necessary based on your pet's lifestyle. There is no doubt that heartworm is a dreadful disease that threatens the lives of dogs. However, the likelihood of your dog's being bitten by an infected mosquito is slim in most places, and a mosquito-repellent (or an herbal remedy such as Wormwood or Black Walnut) is much safer for your dog and will not compromise his immune system (the way heartworm preventatives will). Should you decide to use the traditional preventative "medications," you can consider giving the pill every other or third month. Since the toxins in the pill will kill the heartworms at all stages of development, the pill would be effective in killing larvae, nymphs or adults, and it takes four months for the larvae to reach the adult stage. Thus, there is no rationale to poisoning the dog's system on a monthly basis. Lastly, do not give the pill during the winter months, since there are no mosquitoes around to pass on their infection, unless you live in a tropical environment.

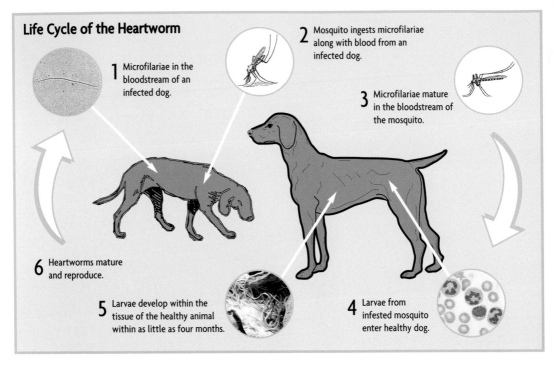

Life Cycle of the Heartworm

1 Microfilariae in the bloodstream of an infected dog.

2 Mosquito ingests microfilariae along with blood from an infected dog.

3 Microfilariae mature in the bloodstream of the mosquito.

4 Larvae from infested mosquito enter healthy dog.

5 Larvae develop within the tissue of the healthy animal within as little as four months.

6 Heartworms mature and reproduce.

HEARTWORMS

Heartworms are thin, extended worms up to 12 inches long, which live in a dog's heart and the major blood vessels surrounding it. Dogs may have up to 200 worms. Symptoms may be loss of energy, loss of appetite, coughing, the development of a pot belly and anemia.

Heartworms are transmitted by mosquitoes. The mosquito drinks the blood of an infected dog and takes in larvae with the blood. The larvae, called microfilariae, develop within the body of the mosquito and are passed on to the next dog bitten after the larvae mature. It takes two to three weeks for the larvae to develop to the infective stage within the body of the mosquito. Dogs are usually treated at about six weeks of age and maintained on a prophylactic dose given monthly.

Blood testing for heartworms is not necessarily indicative of how seriously your dog is infected. Although this is a dangerous disease, it is not easy for a dog to be infected. Discuss the various preventatives with your vet, as there are many different types now available. Together you can decide on a safe course of prevention for your dog.

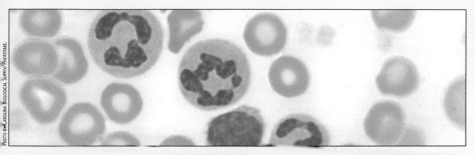

Magnified heart-worm larvae, *Dirofilaria immitis.*

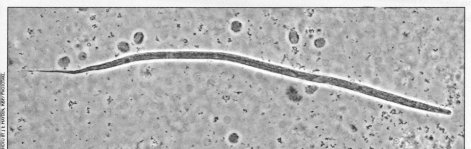

Heartworm, *Dirofilaria immitis.*

The heart of a dog infected with canine heart-worm, *Dirofilaria immitis.*

HOMEOPATHY:
an alternative to conventional medicine

"Less is Most"

Using this principle, the strength of a homeopathic remedy is measured by the number of serial dilutions that were undertaken to create it. The greater the number of serial dilutions, the greater the strength of the homeopathic remedy. The potency of a remedy that has been made by making a dilution of 1 part in 100 parts (or 1/100) is 1c or 1cH. If this remedy is subjected to a series of further dilutions, each one being 1/100, a more dilute and stronger remedy is produced. If the remedy is diluted in this way six times, it is called 6c or 6cH. A dilution of 6c is 1 part in 1,000,000,000,000. In general, higher potencies in more frequent doses are better for acute symptoms and lower potencies in more infrequent doses are more useful for chronic, long-standing problems.

CURING OUR DOGS NATURALLY

Holistic medicine means treating the whole animal as a unique, perfect living being. Generally, holistic treatments do not suppress the symptoms that the body naturally produces, as do most medications prescribed by conventional doctors and vets. Holistic methods seek to cure disease by regaining balance and harmony in the patient's environment. Some of these methods include use of nutritional therapy, herbs, flower essences, aromatherapy, acupuncture, massage, chiropractic and, of course, the most popular holistic approach, homeopathy.

Homeopathy is a theory or system of treating illness with small doses of substances which, if administered in larger quantities, would produce the symptoms that the patient already has. This approach is often described as "like cures like." Although modern veterinary medicine is geared toward the "quick fix," homeopathy relies on the belief that, given the time, the body is able to heal itself and return to its natural, healthy state.

Choosing a remedy to cure a problem in our dogs is the difficult part of homeopathy. Consult with your vet for a professional diagnosis of your dog's symptoms. Often

these symptoms require immediate conventional care. If your vet is willing and knowledgeable, you may attempt a homeopathic remedy. Be aware that cortisone prevents homeopathic remedies from working. There are hundreds of possibilities and combinations to cure many problems in dogs, from basic physical problems such as excessive shedding, fleas or other parasites, unattractive doggy odor, bad breath, upset tummy, obesity, dry, oily or dull coat, diarrhea, ear problems or eye discharge (including tears and dry or mucousy matter), to behavioral abnormalities such as fear of loud noises, habitual licking, poor appetite, excessive barking and various phobias. From alumina to zincum metallicum, the remedies span the planet and the imagination...from flowers and weeds to chemicals, insect droppings, diesel smoke and volcanic ash.

Using "Like to Treat Like"

Unlike conventional medicines that suppress symptoms, homeopathic remedies treat illnesses with small doses of substances that, if administered in larger quantities, would produce the symptoms that the patient already has. While the same homeopathic remedy can be used to treat different symptoms in different dogs, here are some interesting remedies and their uses.

Apis Mellifica
(made from honey bee venom) can be used for allergies or to reduce swelling that occurs in acutely infected kidneys.

Diesel Smoke
can be used to help control travel sickness.

Calcarea Fluorica
(made from calcium fluoride, which helps harden bone structure) can be useful in treating hard lumps in tissues.

Natrum Muriaticum
(made from common salt, sodium chloride) is useful in treating thin, thirsty dogs.

Nitricum Acidum
(made from nitric acid) is used for symptoms you would expect to see from contact with acids, such as lesions, especially where the skin joins the linings of body orifices or openings such as the lips and nostrils.

Symphytum
(made from the herb Knitbone, *Symphytum officianale*) is used to encourage bones to heal.

Urtica Urens
(made from the common stinging nettle) is used in treating painful, irritating rashes.

HOMEOPATHIC REMEDIES FOR YOUR DOG

Symptom/Ailment	Possible Remedy
ALLERGIES	Apis Mellifica 30c, Astacus Fluviatilis 6c, Pulsatilla 30c, Urtica Urens 6c
ALOPECIA	Alumina 30c, Lycopodium 30c, Sepia 30c, Thallium 6c
ANAL GLANDS (BLOCKED)	Hepar Sulphuris Calcareum 30c, Sanicula 6c, Silicea 6c
ARTHRITIS	Rhus Toxicodendron 6c, Bryonia Alba 6c
CATARACT	Calcarea Carbonica 6c, Conium Maculatum 6c, Phosphorus 30c, Silicea 30c
CONSTIPATION	Alumina 6c, Carbo Vegetabilis 30c, Graphites 6c, Nitricum Acidum 30c, Silicea 6c
COUGHING	Aconitum Napellus 6c, Belladonna 30c, Hyoscyamus Niger 30c, Phosphorus 30c
DIARRHEA	Arsenicum Album 30c, Aconitum Napellus 6c, Chamomilla 30c, Mercurius Corrosivus 30c
DRY EYE	Zincum Metallicum 30c
EAR PROBLEMS	Aconitum Napellus 30c, Belladonna 30c, Hepar Sulphuris 30c, Tellurium 30c, Psorinum 200c
EYE PROBLEMS	Borax 6c, Aconitum Napellus 30c, Graphites 6c, Staphysagria 6c, Thuja Occidentalis 30c
GLAUCOMA	Aconitum Napellus 30c, Apis Mellifica 6c, Phosphorus 30c
HEAT STROKE	Belladonna 30c, Gelsemium Sempervirens 30c, Sulphur 30c
HICCOUGHS	Cinchona Deficinalis 6c
HIP DYSPLASIA	Colocynthis 6c, Rhus Toxicodendron 6c, Bryonia Alba 6c
INCONTINENCE	Argentum Nitricum 6c, Causticum 30c, Conium Maculatum 30c, Pulsatilla 30c, Sepia 30c
INSECT BITES	Apis Mellifica 30c, Cantharis 30c, Hypericum Perforatum 6c, Urtica Urens 30c
ITCHING	Alumina 30c, Arsenicum Album 30c, Carbo Vegetabilis 30c, Hypericum Perforatum 6c, Mezerium 6c, Sulphur 30c
KENNEL COUGH	Drosera 6c, Ipecacuanha 30c
MASTITIS	Apis Mellifica 30c, Belladonna 30c, Urtica Urens 1m
MOTION SICKNESS	Cocculus 6c, Petroleum 6c
PATELLAR LUXATION	Gelsemium Sempervirens 6c, Rhus Toxicodendron 6c
PENIS PROBLEMS	Aconitum Napellus 30c, Hepar Sulphuris Calcareum 30c, Pulsatilla 30c, Thuja Occidentalis 6c
PUPPY TEETHING	Calcarea Carbonica 6c, Chamomilla 6c, Phytolacca 6c

Recognizing a Sick Dog

Unlike colicky babies and cranky children, our canine kids cannot tell us when they are feeling ill. Therefore, there are a number of signs that owners can identify to know that their dogs are not feeling well.

Take note for physical manifestations such as:

- unusual, bad odor, including bad breath
- excessive shedding
- wax in the ears, chronic ear irritation
- oily, flaky, dull haircoat
- mucus, tearing or similar discharge in the eyes
- fleas or mites
- mucus in stool, diarrhea
- sensitivity to petting or handling
- licking at paws, scratching face, etc.

Keep an eye out for behavioral changes as well including:

- lethargy, idleness
- lack of patience or general irritability
- lack of appetite
- phobias (fear of people, loud noises, etc.)
- strange behavior, suspicion, fear
- coprophagia
- more frequent barking
- whimpering, crying

Get Well Soon

You don't need a DVM to provide good TLC to your sick or recovering dog, but you do need to pay attention to some details that normally wouldn't bother him. The following tips will aid Fido's recovery and get him back on his paws again:

- Keep his space free of irritating smells, like heavy perfumes and air fresheners.
- Rest is the best medicine! Avoid harsh lighting that will prevent your dog from sleeping. Shade him from bright sunlight during the day and dim the lights in the evening.
- Keep the noise level down. Animals are more sensitive to sound when they are sick.

- Be attentive to any necessary temperature adjustments. A dog with a fever needs a cool room and cold liquids. A bitch that is whelping or recovering from surgery will be more comfortable in a warm room, consuming warm liquids and food.
- You wouldn't send a sick child back to school early, so don't rush your dog back into a full routine until he seems absolutely ready.

TOY FOX TERRIER

Depending on with which national club you have registered your Toy Fox Terrier, you should consider exhibiting your dog, especially if the breeder has assured you that the puppy is a promising show prospect. This chapter will explain how dog shows operate for shows sponsored by the American Kennel Club and the United Kennel Club, the two largest all-breed clubs in the US. Many pet owners enter their "average" TFTs in dog shows for the fun and enjoyment of it. Dog showing makes an absorbing hobby, with many rewards for dogs and owners alike. If you're having fun, meeting other people who share your interests and enjoying the overall experience, you likely will catch the "bug."

AKC DOG SHOWS
Visiting a dog show as a spectator is a great place to start. Pick up the show catalog to find out what time your breed is being shown, who is judging the breed and in which ring the classes will be held. To start, Toy Fox Terriers compete against other Toy Fox Terriers, and the winner is selected as Best of Breed by the judge. This is the

BECOMING A CHAMPION
An official AKC championship of record requires that a dog accumulate 15 points under three different judges, including two "majors" under different judges. Points are awarded based on the number of dogs entered into competition, varying from breed to breed and place to place. A win of three, four or five points is considered a "major." The AKC annually assigns a schedule of points to adjust for variations that accompany a breed's popularity and the population of a given area.

procedure for each breed. At a group show, all of the Best of Breed winners go on to compete for Group One in their respective group. For example, all Best of Breed winners in a given group compete against each other; this is done for all seven groups. Finally, all seven group winners go head to head in the ring for the Best in Show award.

What most spectators don't understand is the basic idea of conformation. A dog show is often referred as a "conformation" show.

This means that the judge should decide how each dog stacks up (conforms) to the breed standard for his given breed: how well does this Toy Fox Terrier conform to the ideal representative detailed in the standard? Ideally, this is what happens. In reality, however, this ideal often gets slighted as the judge compares Toy Fox Terrier #1 to Toy Fox Terrier #2. Again, the ideal is that each dog is judged based on his merits in comparison to his breed standard, not in comparison to the other dogs in the ring. It is easier for judges to compare dogs of the same breed to decide which they think is the better specimen; in the Group and Best in Show ring, however, it is very difficult to compare one breed to another, like apples to oranges.

Thus the dog's conformation to the breed standard is essential to success in conformation shows. The dog described in the standard is the perfect dog of that breed, and breeders keep their eye on the standard when they choose which dogs to breed, hoping to get closer and closer to the ideal with each litter.

Three kinds of conformation shows are offered by the AKC. There is the all-breed show, in which all AKC-recognized breeds can compete; the specialty show, which is for one breed only and usually sponsored by the breed's parent club and the group show, for all breeds in one of the AKC's seven groups. The Toy Fox Terrier competes in the Toy Group.

For a dog to become an AKC

The judge evaluates the dogs' gait as the handlers walk them around the ring. Correct movement translates to proper structure for every breed.

Socialization pays off in the show ring as well. Your Toy Fox Terrier must be friendly and outgoing to the judge, who would penalize the dog for being shy or aggressive.

champion of record, the dog must earn 15 points at shows. The points must be awarded by at least three different judges and must include two "majors" under different judges. A "major" is a three-, four- or five-point win, and the number of points per win is determined by the number of dogs competing in the show on that day. (Dogs that are absent or are excused are not counted.) The number of points that are awarded varies from breed to breed. More dogs are needed to attain a major in more popular breeds, and fewer dogs are needed in less popular breeds. Yearly, the AKC evaluates the number of dogs in competition in each division (there are 14 divisions in all, based on geography) and may or may not change the numbers of dogs required for

each number of points.

Only one dog and one bitch of each breed can win points at a given show. Dogs and bitches do not compete against each other until they are champions. Dogs that are not champions (referred to as "class dogs") compete in one of five classes. The class in which a dog is entered depends on age and previous show wins. First there is the Puppy Class (sometimes divided further into classes for 6- to 9-month-olds and 9- to 12-month-olds); next is the Novice Class (for dogs that have no points toward their championship and whose only first-place wins have come in the Puppy Class or the Novice Class, the latter class limited to three first places); then there is the American-bred Class (for dogs bred in the US); the Bred-by-Exhibitor Class (for dogs handled by their breeders or by immediate family members of their breeders) and the Open Class (for any non-champions). Any dog may enter the Open Class, regardless of age or win history, but to be competitive the dog should be older and have ring experience.

The judge at the show begins judging the male dogs in the Puppy Class(es) and proceeds through the other classes. The judge awards first through fourth place in each class. The first-place winners of each class then compete with one another in the Winners Class to determine

Winners Dog. The judge then starts over with the bitches, beginning with the Puppy Class(es) and proceeding up to the Winners Class to award Winners Bitch, just as he did with the dogs. A Reserve Winners Dog and Reserve Winners Bitch are also selected; they could be awarded the points in the case of a disqualification.

The Winners Dog and Winners Bitch are the two that are awarded the points for their breed. They then go on to compete with any champions of record (often called "specials") of their breed that are entered in the show. The champions may be dogs or bitches; in this class, all are shown together. The judge reviews the Winners Dog and Winners Bitch along with all of the champions to select the Best of Breed winner. The Best of Winners is selected between the Winners Dog and Winners Bitch; if one of these two is selected Best of Breed as well, he or she is automatically determined Best of Winners. Lastly, the judge selects Best of Opposite Sex to the Best of Breed winner. The Best of Breed winner then goes on to the Group competition.

At a Group or all-breed show, the Best of Breed winners from each breed are divided into their respective groups to compete against one another for Group One through Group Four. Group One (first place) is awarded to the dog that best lives up to the ideal for his breed as described in the standard. A Group judge, therefore, must have a thorough working knowledge of many breed standards. After placements have been

CLUB CONTACTS

You can get information about dog shows from the national kennel clubs:

American Kennel Club
5580 Centerview Dr., Raleigh, NC 27606-3390
www.akc.org

United Kennel Club
100 E. Kilgore Road, Kalamazoo, MI 49002
www.ukcdogs.com

Canadian Kennel Club
89 Skyway Ave., Suite 100, Etobicoke,
Ontario M9W 6R4 Canada
www.ckc.ca

The Kennel Club
1-5 Clarges St., Piccadilly,
London W1Y 8AB, UK
www.the-kennel-club.org.uk

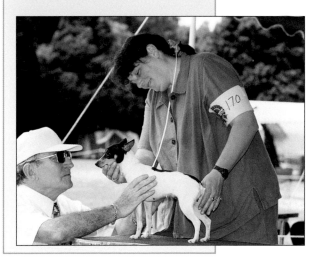

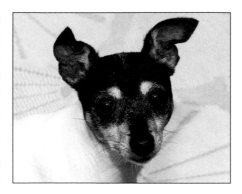

made in each Group, the seven Group One winners (from the Sporting Group, Toy Group, Hound Group, etc.) compete against each other for the top honor, Best in Show.

UKC DOG SHOWS

UKC dog shows may be held for one breed only, several breeds or all breeds. UKC shows are arranged differently from the conformation shows of other organizations. Entries are restricted by age, and you cannot show your dog in a class other than his correct age class. When you compete for championship points, you may enter Puppy (6-12 months), Junior (1-2 years), Senior (2-3 years) or Adult (3 years and older). You may also enter the Breeder/Handler Class, where dogs of all ages compete, but the dog must be handled by his breeder or a member of the breeder's immediate family. The winners of each class compete for Best Male or Best Female. These two dogs then

compete for Best of Winners; the dog who is given this award will go on to compete for Best of Breed. Best of Breed competition includes the Best of Winners and dogs that have earned Champion and Grand Champion titles. Earning Best Male or Best Female, as long as there is competition, is considered a "major."

Once a dog has earned three "majors" and accumulated 100 points, he is considered a UKC champion. What this means is that the dog is now ready to compete for the title of Grand Champion, which is equivalent to an AKC championship. To earn the Grand Champion title, a dog must compete with a minimum of two other dogs who are also champions. The dog must win this class, called the Champion of Champions class, five times under three different judges. In rare breeds, it is difficult to assemble a class of champions, so the UKC Grand Champion title is truly a prestigious one. Once a dog has earned the Grand Champion title, he can continue to compete for Top Ten, but there are no further titles to earn. "Top Ten" refers to the ten dogs in each breed that have won the most points in a given year. These dogs compete in a Top Ten invitational competition annually.

The breeds recognized by the UKC are divided into groups. The Toy Fox Terrier competes in the Terrier Group, which consists of

AMERICA'S ALTERNATIVE: THE UNITED KENNEL CLUB

The United Kennel Club defines itself as follows: "With 250,000 registrations annually, the United Kennel Club is the second oldest and second largest all breed dog registry in the United States. Founded in 1898 by Chauncey Z. Bennett, the registry has always supported the idea of the 'total dog,' meaning a dog that looks and performs equally well. The performance programs of UKC include Conformation Shows, Obedience Trials, Agility Trials, Coonhound Field Trials, Water Races, Nite Hunts and Bench Shows, hunting tests for the retrieving breeds, beagle events including Hunts and Bench Shows, and, for Cur and Feist, Squirrel and Coon Events, and Bench Shows. Essentially, the UKC world of dogs is a working world. That's the way founder Chauncey Bennett designed it, and that's the way it remains today."

dogs of earth-dog and bull-and-terrier origins. Depending on the show-giving club, group competition may or may not be offered. A group must have a minimum of five breeds entered in order for group competition to take place. If group competition is offered, Best in Show consists of the group winners. If there is no group competition, then all Best of Breed dogs go into the ring at the same time to compete for Best in Show.

This can be a large number of dogs and thus can be very interesting, to say the least!

Aside from the variations already presented, UKC shows differ from other dog shows in one very significant way: no professional handlers are allowed to show dogs, except for those dogs they own themselves. UKC shows create an atmosphere that is owner-friendly, relaxed and genuinely fun. Bait in the ring is allowed at the discretion of the judge, but throwing the bait, dropping it on the floor or other "handler tricks" will get an owner excused from the ring in a big hurry.

In addition to dog shows, the UKC offers many, many more venues for dogs and their owners, in keeping with its mission of promoting the "total dog." UKC obedience events test the training of dogs as they perform a series of prescribed exercises at the commands of their handlers. There are several levels of competition, ranging from basic commands such as "sit," "come" and "heel," to advanced exercises like scent discrimination and directed retrieves over jumps, based on the dog's level of accomplishment. The classes are further delineated by the experience of the handler.

OBEDIENCE TRIALS

Any dog that is registered, regardless of neutering or other disquali-

Not limited by his size, the Toy Fox Terrier can bound over many obstacles. The breed does very well in agility trials.

fications that would preclude entry in conformation competition, can participate in obedience trials. There are three levels of difficulty in AKC obedience competition. The first (and easiest) level is the Novice, in which dogs can earn the Companion Dog (CD) title. The intermediate level is the Open level, in which the Companion Dog Excellent (CDX) title is awarded. The advanced level is the Utility level, in which dogs compete for the Utility Dog (UD) title. Classes at each level are further divided into "A" and "B," with "A" for beginners and "B" for those with more experience. In order to win a title at a given level,

a dog must earn three "legs." A "leg" is accomplished when a dog scores 170 or higher (200 is a perfect score). The scoring system gets a little trickier when you understand that a dog must score more than 50% of the points available for each exercise in order to actually earn the points. Available points for each exercise range between 20 and 40.

A dog must complete different exercises at each level of obedience. The Novice exercises are the easiest, with the Open and finally the Utility levels progressing in difficulty. Examples of Novice exercises are on- and off-lead heeling, a figure-8 pattern, performing a recall (or come), long sit and long down and standing for examination. In the Open level, the Novice-level exercises are required again, but this time without a leash and for longer durations. In addition, the dog must clear a broad jump, retrieve over a jump and drop on recall. In the Utility level, the exercises are quite difficult, including executing basic commands based on hand signals, following a complex heeling pattern, locating articles based on scent discrimination and completing jumps at the handler's direction.

Once he's earned the UD title, a dog can go on to win the prestigious title of Utility Dog Excellent (UDX) by winning "legs" in ten shows. Additionally, Utility Dogs who win "legs" in Open B and

Utility B earn points toward the lofty title of Obedience Trial Champion (OTCh.).

UKC obedience differs from AKC obedience in many respects. Even at the most basic levels, the dogs are expected to "honor" other dogs who are working. In other words, the "honoring" dog must be placed in a down-stay while his owner leaves the ring and moves out of sight. The dog must remain in the down-stay position while the working dog goes through the heeling exercises.

AGILITY TRIALS

Agility events are fast-paced exercises in which the handler directs his dog through a course involving tunnels, sway bridges, jumps and other obstacles in a race against the clock. The dogs are scored according to the manner in which they negotiate the obstacles and the time elapsed to complete the course. Agility trials became sanctioned by the AKC in August 1994, when the first licensed agility trials were held. The AKC allows all registered breeds to participate, providing the dog is 12 months of age or older. Agility is designed so that the handler demonstrates how well the dog can work at his side. The handler directs his dog through, over, under and around an obstacle course that includes jumps, tires, the dog walk, weave poles, pipe tunnels, collapsed tunnels and more. While working

his way through the course, the dog must keep one eye and ear on the handler and the rest of his body on the course. The handler runs along with the dog, giving verbal and hand signals to guide the dog through the course. UKC agility is very similar to AKC agility; clubs often will offer both AKC and UKC agility events (not on the same day).

The first organization to promote agility trials in the US was the United States Dog Agility Association, Inc. (USDAA). Established in 1986, the USDAA sparked the formation of many member clubs around the country. To participate in USDAA trials, dogs must be at least 18 months of age. All three clubs offer titles to winning dogs, although the exercises and requirements of the two organizations differ.

Agility trials are a great way to keep your dog active, and they will keep you running, too! You should join a local agility club to learn more about the sport. These clubs offer sessions in which you can introduce your dog to the various obstacles as well as training classes to prepare him for competition. In no time, your dog will be climbing A-frames, crossing the dog walk and flying over hurdles, all with you right beside him. Your heart will leap every time your dog jumps through the hoop—and you'll be having just as much (if not more) fun!

THINK LIKE A DOG

Dogs do not think like humans, nor do humans think like dogs, though we try. Unfortunately, a dog is incapable of comprehending how humans think, so the responsibility falls on the owner to adopt a viable canine mindset. Dogs cannot rationalize, and they exist in the present moment. Many a dog owner makes the mistake in training of thinking that he can reprimand his dog for something that the dog did a while ago. Basically, you cannot even reprimand a dog for something he did 20 seconds ago! Either catch him in the act or forget it! It is a waste of your and your dog's time—in his mind, you are reprimanding him for whatever he is doing at that moment.

The following behavioral problems represent some that owners most commonly encounter. Every dog is unique and every situation is unique. No author could purport for you to solve your Toy Fox Terrier's problems simply by reading a chapter in a breed book. Here we outline some basic "dogspeak" so that owners' chances of solving behavioral problems are increased.

> **AIN'T MISBEHAVIN'**
> Punishment is rarely necessary for a misbehaving dog. Dogs that habitually behave badly probably had a poor education and do not know what is expected of them. They need training. Negative reinforcement on your part usually does more harm than good.

Discuss bad habits with your veterinarian and he can recommend a behavioral specialist to consult in appropriate cases. Since behavioral abnormalities are the main reason for owners' abandoning their pets, we hope that you will make a valiant effort to solve your Toy Fox Terrier's problems. Patience and understanding are virtues that must dwell in every pet-loving household.

SEPARATION ANXIETY

Recognized by behaviorists as the most common form of stress for dogs, separation anxiety can also lead to destructive behaviors in your dog. It's more than your Toy Fox Terrier's howling his displeasure at your leaving the house and his being left alone. This is a normal reaction, no different than the child who cries as his mother leaves him on the first day at school. Separation anxiety, however, is more serious. In fact, if you are constantly with your dog, he will come to expect you with him all of the time, making it even more traumatic for him when you are not there.

Obviously, you enjoy spending time with your dog, and he thrives on your love and attention. However, it should not become a dependent relationship in which he is heartbroken without you. This broken heart can also bring on destructive behavior as well as loss of appetite, depression and lack of interest in play and interaction. Canine behaviorists have been spending much time and energy to help owners better understand the significance of this stressful condition.

One thing you can do to minimize separation anxiety is to make your entrances and exits as low-key as possible. Do not give your dog a long drawn-out goodbye, and do not lavish him with hugs and kisses when you return. This is giving in to the attention that he craves, and it will only make him miss it more when you are away. Another thing you can try is to give your dog a treat when you leave; this will not only keep him occupied and keep his mind off the fact that you have just left, but it will also help

him associate your leaving with a pleasant experience.

You may have to accustom your dog to being left alone in intervals. Of course, when your dog starts whimpering as you approach the door, your first instinct will be to run to him and comfort him, but do not do it! Eventually he will adjust to your absence. His anxiety stems from being placed in an unfamiliar situation; by familiarizing him with

Oftentimes a dominant dog will not share his bed with any other pet, especially the family cat. Fortunately, most Toy Fox Terriers are easygoing and amicable.

I'M HOME!
Dogs left alone for varying lengths of time may often react wildly when their owners return. Sometimes they run, jump, bite, chew, tear things apart, wet themselves, gobble their food or behave in very undisciplined ways. If your dog behaves in this manner upon your return home, allow him to calm down before greeting him or he will consider your attention as a reward for his antics.

BELLY UP!
When two dogs are introduced, they will naturally establish who is dominant. This may involve one dog placing his front paws on the other's shoulders, or one dog rolling over and exposing his belly, thereby assuming a submissive status. If neither dog submits, they may fight until one has been pinned down. The biggest mistake you can make is to interfere, pulling on the leads and confusing the dogs. If you don't allow them to establish their pecking order, you undermine the pack mentality, which can cause your dog great stress. If you separate dogs in the middle of a fight, the interference may incite them to attack each other viciously. Your best choice is to stay out of it!

being alone, he will learn that he will survive. That is not to say you should purposely leave your dog home alone, but the dog needs to know that, while he can depend on you for his care, you do not have to be by his side 24 hours a day. Some behaviorists recommend tiring the dog out before you leave home—take him for a good long walk or engage in a game of fetch in the yard.

When the dog is alone in the house, he should be placed in his crate—another distinct advantage to crate-training your dog. The crate should be placed in his familiar happy family area, where he normally sleeps and already feels comfortable, thereby making him feel more at ease when he is alone. Be sure to give the dog a special chew toy to enjoy while he settles into his crate.

AGGRESSION
This is a problem that concerns all responsible dog owners.

Aggression can be a very big problem in dogs, and, when not controlled, always becomes dangerous. An aggressive dog, no matter the size, may lunge at, bite or even attack a person or another dog. Aggressive behavior is not to be tolerated. It is more than just inappropriate behavior; it is painful for a family to watch their dog become unpredictable in his behavior to the point where they are afraid of him. While not all aggressive behavior is dangerous, growling, baring teeth, etc., can be frightening. It is important to ascertain why the dog is acting in this manner. Aggression is a display of dominance, and the dog should not have the dominant role in his pack, which is, in this case, your family.

It is important not to challenge an aggressive dog, as this could provoke an attack. Observe your Toy Fox Terrier's body language. Does he make direct eye contact and stare? Does he try to make himself as large as possible: ears pricked, chest out, tail erect? Height and size signify authority in a dog pack—being taller or "above" another dog literally means that he is "above" in social status. These body signals tell you that your Toy Fox Terrier thinks he is in charge, a problem that needs to be addressed. An aggressive dog is unpredictable; you never know when he is going to strike and what he is going to do. You cannot understand why a dog that is playful one minute is growling the next.

Fear is a common cause of aggression in dogs. Perhaps your Toy Fox Terrier had a negative experience as a puppy, which causes him to be fearful when a similar situation presents itself later in life. The dog may act aggressively in order to protect himself from whatever is making him afraid. It is not always easy to determine what is making your dog fearful, but if you can isolate what brings out the fear reaction, you can help the dog get over it.

Supervise your Toy Fox Terrier's interactions with people and other dogs, and praise the dog when it goes well. If he starts to act aggressively in a situation, correct him and remove him from the situation. Do not let people approach the dog and start petting him without your express permission. That way, you can have the dog sit to accept petting, and praise him when he behaves properly. You are focusing on praise and on modifying his behavior by rewarding him when he acts appropriately. By being gentle and by supervising his interactions, you are showing him that there is no need to be afraid or defensive.

The best solution is to consult a behavioral specialist, one who has experience with the Toy Fox Terrier if possible. Together, perhaps you can pinpoint the cause of your dog's aggression and do something about it. An aggressive dog cannot be trusted, and a dog that cannot be trusted is not safe to have as a family pet. If, very unusually, you find that your pet has become untrustworthy and you feel it necessary to seek a new home with a more suitable family and environment, explain fully to the new owners all your reasons for rehoming the dog to be fair to all concerned.

SEXUAL BEHAVIOR
Dogs exhibit certain sexual behaviors that may have influenced your choice of male or female when you first purchased your Toy Fox Terrier. To a certain extent, spaying/neutering will eliminate these behaviors, but if you are purchasing a dog that you wish to breed from, you should be aware of what you will have to deal with throughout the dog's life.

Sexual behavior goes beyond the act of mating. Mounting is commonly seen in males and females alike and is usually a gesture of dominance.

Female dogs usually have two estruses per year, with each season lasting about three weeks. These are the only times in which a female dog will mate, and she usually will not allow this until the second week of the cycle, although this varies from bitch to bitch. If not bred during the heat cycle, it is not uncommon for a bitch to experience a false pregnancy, in which her mammary glands swell and she exhibits maternal tendencies toward toys or other objects.

With male dogs, owners must be aware that whole dogs (dogs who are not neutered) have the natural inclination to mark their territory. Males mark their territory by spraying small amounts of urine as they lift their legs in a macho ritual. Marking can occur both outdoors in the yard and around the neighborhood as well as indoors on furniture legs, curtains and the sofa. Such behavior can be very frustrating for the owner; early training is strongly urged before the "urge" strikes your dog. Neutering the male at an appropriate early age can solve this problem before it becomes a habit.

Other problems associated with males are wandering and mounting. Both of these habits, of course, belong to the unneutered dog, whose sexual drive leads him away from home in search of the bitch in heat. Males will mount females in heat, as well as any other dog, male or female, that happens to catch their fancy. Other possible mounting partners include his owner, the furniture, guests to the home and strangers on the street. Discourage such behavior early on.

Owners must further recognize that mounting is not merely a sexual expression but also one of dominance, seen in males and females alike. Be consistent and be persistent, and you will find that you can "move mounters."

CHEWING
The national canine pastime is chewing! Every dog loves to sink his "canines" into a tasty bone, so it is important to provide your dog with appropriate chew toys so that he doesn't destroy your possessions or make a habit of gnawing on your hands and fingers. Dogs

need to chew to massage their gums, to make their new teeth feel better and to exercise their jaws, and the Toy Fox is a breed that enjoys chewing. This is a natural behavior that is deeply embedded in all things canine. Your role as owner is not to stop the dog's chewing, but rather to redirect it to positive, chew-worthy objects. Be an informed owner and purchase proper chew toys, like strong nylon bones, that will not splinter. Be sure that the objects are safe and durable, since your dog's safety is at risk. Again, the owner is responsible for ensuring a dog-proof environment.

The best answer is prevention; that is, put your shoes, handbags and other tasty objects in their proper places (out of the reach of the growing canine mouth). Direct your puppy to his toys whenever you see him "tasting" the furniture legs or the leg of your pants. Make a loud noise to attract the pup's attention and immediately escort him to his chew toy and engage him with the toy for at least four minutes, praising and encouraging him all the while. An array of safe, interesting chew toys will keep your dog's mind and teeth occupied, and distracted from chewing on things he shouldn't.

Some trainers recommend deterrents, such as hot pepper, a bitter spice or a product designed for this purpose, to discourage the dog from chewing forbidden objects. Test these products to see which works best before investing in large quantities.

JUMPING UP
Jumping up is a dog's friendly way of saying hello! Some dog owners do not mind when their dog jumps up. The problem arises when guests come to the house and the dog greets them in the same manner—whether they like it or not! However friendly the greeting may be, and despite the Toy Fox's small size, chances are that your visitors will not appreciate your

"X" MARKS THE SPOT
As a pack animal, your dog marks his territory as a way of letting any possible intruders know that this is his space and that he will defend his territory if necessary. Your dog marks by urinating because urine contains pheromones that allow other canines to identify him. While this behavior seems like a nuisance, it speaks volumes about your dog's mental health. Stable, well-trained dogs living in quiet, less populated areas may mark less frequently than less confident dogs inhabiting busy urban areas that attract many possible invaders. If your dog only marks in certain areas in your home, your bed or just the front door, these are the areas he feels obligated to defend. If your dog marks frequently, see your veterinarian or an animal behaviorist.

The "terrier" in the breed's name refers to its earth-dog origins. Digging is one of the Toy Fox Terrier's favorite talents.

dog's enthusiasm. The dog will not be able to distinguish upon whom he can jump and whom he cannot. Therefore, it is probably best to discourage this behavior entirely.

Pick a command such as "Off" (avoid using "Down" since you will use that for the dog to lie down) and tell him "Off" when he jumps up. Place him on the ground on all fours and have him sit, praising him the whole time. Always lavish him with praise and petting when he is in the sit position. In this way, you can give him a warm affectionate greeting, let him know that you are as pleased to see him as he is to see you and instill good manners at the same time!

DIGGING

Digging, which is seen as a destructive behavior to humans, is actually quite a natural behavior in dogs. Although a toy breed, your Toy Fox is still one of the "earth dogs" (also known as terriers), and these breeds are most

associated with digging. The Toy Fox Terrier loves to "go to ground," and his desire to dig can be irrepressible and most frustrating to his owners.

When digging occurs in your yard, it is actually a normal behavior redirected into something the dog can do in his everyday life. In the wild, a dog would be actively seeking food, making his own shelter, etc. He would be using his paws in a purposeful manner for his survival. Since you provide him with food and shelter, he has no need to use his paws for these purposes, and so the energy that he would be using may manifest itself in the form of little holes all over your yard and flower beds.

Perhaps your dog is digging as a reaction to boredom—it is somewhat similar to someone eating a whole bag of chips in front of the TV—because they are there and there is nothing better to do! Basically, the answer is to provide the dog with adequate play and exercise so that his mind and paws are occupied, and so that he feels as if he is doing something useful.

Of course, digging is easiest to control if it is stopped as soon as possible, but it is often hard to catch a dog in the act. If your dog is a compulsive digger and is not easily distracted by other activities, you can designate an area on your property where he is allowed to dig. If you catch him digging in an off-limits area of the garden, immediately take him to the approved area and praise him for digging there. Keep a close eye on him so that you can catch him in the act—that is the only way to make him understand what is permitted and what is not. If you take him to a hole he dug an hour ago and tell him "No," he will understand that you are not fond of holes, dirt or flowers. If you catch him while he is stifle-deep in your tulips, that is when he will get your message.

BARKING

Barking is a dog's way of "talking." It can be somewhat frustrating because it is not always easy to tell what a dog means by his bark—is he excited, happy, frightened or angry? Whatever it is that the dog is trying to say, he should not be punished for barking. It is only when the barking becomes excessive, and when the excessive barking becomes a bad habit, that the behavior needs to be modified.

If an intruder came into your home in the middle of the night and your Toy Fox Terrier barked a warning, wouldn't you be pleased? You would probably deem your dog a hero, a wonderful guardian and protector of the home. On the other hand, if a friend drops by unexpectedly, rings the doorbell and is greeted with a sudden sharp bark, you would probably be annoyed at the dog. But in reality,

isn't this just the same behavior? The dog does not know any better. Unless he sees who is at the door and it is someone he knows, he will bark as a means of vocalizing that his (and your) territory is being threatened. While your friend is not posing a threat, it is all the same to the dog. Barking is his means of letting you know that there is an intrusion, whether

> ## HE'S PROTECTING YOU
> If your dog barks at a stranger walking past your house, a moving car or a fleeing cat, he is merely exercising his responsibility to protect his pack (*you*) and territory from a perceived intruder. Since the "intruder" usually keeps going, the dog thinks his barking chased it away and he feels fulfilled. This behavior leads your overly vocal friend to believe that he is in charge.

friend or foe, on your property. This type of barking is instinctive and should not be discouraged.

However, Toy Fox Terriers can become nuisance barkers if not properly trained early on. As your Toy Fox Terrier grows up, you will be able to tell when his barking is purposeful and when it is for no reason. You will become able to distinguish your dog's different barks and their meanings. For example, the bark when someone comes to the door will be different from the bark when he is excited to see you. It is similar to a person's tone of voice, except that the dog has to rely totally on tone of voice because he does not have the benefit of using words. An incessant barker will be evident at an early age.

There are some things that encourage a dog to bark. For example, if your dog barks non-stop for a few minutes and you give him a treat to quiet him, he believes that you are rewarding him for barking. He will associate barking with getting a treat and will keep doing it until he is rewarded. On the other hand, if you give him a command such as "Quiet" and praise him after he has stopped barking for a few seconds, he will get the idea that being "quiet" is what you want him to do.

FOOD STEALING

Is your dog devising ways of stealing food from your coffee table or kitchen counter? If so, you must answer the following questions: Is your Toy Fox Terrier a bit hungry, or is he "constantly famished" like many dogs seem to be? Face it, some dogs are more food-motivated than others. They are totally obsessed by the smell of food and can only think of their next meal. Food stealing is terrific fun and always yields a great reward—*food*.

Your goal as an owner, therefore, is to be sensible about where food is placed in the home and to reprimand your dog whenever he is caught in the act of stealing. But remember, only reprimand your dog if you actually see him stealing, not later when the crime is discovered; that will be of no use at all and will only serve to confuse him.

BEGGING

Just like food stealing, begging is a favorite pastime of hungry puppies! It achieves that same lovely result—*food!* Dogs quickly learn that their owners keep the "good food" for themselves, and that we humans do not dine on dry food alone. Begging is a conditioned response related to a specific stimulus, time and place. The sounds of the kitchen, cans and bottles opening, crinkling bags, the smell of food in preparation, etc., will excite the dog, and soon the paws will be in the air!

Here is the solution to stopping this behavior: Never give in to a beggar! You are rewarding the dog for sitting pretty, jumping up, whining and rubbing his nose into you by giving him food. By ignoring the dog, you will (eventually) force the behavior into extinction. Note that the behavior is likely to get worse before it disappears, so be sure there are not any "softies" in the family who will give in to little "Oliver" every time he whimpers, "More, please."

COPROPHAGIA

Feces eating is, to humans, one of the most disgusting behaviors that our dogs could engage in; yet, to dogs, it is perfectly normal. It is hard for us to understand why a dog would want to eat his own feces. He could be seeking certain nutrients that are missing from his diet, he could be just hungry or he could be attracted by the pleasing (to a dog) scent. While coprophagia most often refers to the dog's eating his own feces, a dog may just as likely eat that of another animal as well if he comes across it. Dogs often find the stool of cats and horses more palatable than that of other dogs.

Vets have found that diets with low levels of digestibility, containing relatively low levels of fiber and high levels of starch, increase coprophagia. Therefore, high-fiber diets may decrease the likelihood of dogs' eating feces. Both the consistency of the stool (how firm it feels in the dog's

mouth) and the presence of undigested nutrients increase the likelihood. Once the dog develops diarrhea from feces eating, he will likely stop this distasteful habit.

To discourage this behavior, first make sure that the food you are feeding your dog is nutritionally complete and that he is getting enough food. If changes in his diet do not seem to work, and no medical cause can be found, you will have to modify the behavior through environmental control before it becomes a habit. The best way to prevent your dog from eating his stool is to make it unavailable—clean up after he eliminates and remove any stool from the yard.

Reprimanding for stool eating rarely impresses the dog. Vets recommend distracting the dog while he is in the act of stool eating. Coprophagia is seen most frequently in pups 6 to 12 months of age, and usually disappears around the dog's first birthday.

Who can explain the allure of the litter tray? If your dog fancies feline droppings, keep him away from the litter tray and keep the litter tray as clean as possible.

INDEX

My Toy Fox Terrier

PUT YOUR PUPPY'S FIRST PICTURE HERE

Dog's Name _____

Date _____ Photographer _____